Models for Neural Spike Computation and Cognition

David H. Staelin and Carl H. Staelin

First printing: November 2011

Copyright © 2011 by David H. Staelin and Carl H. Staelin.

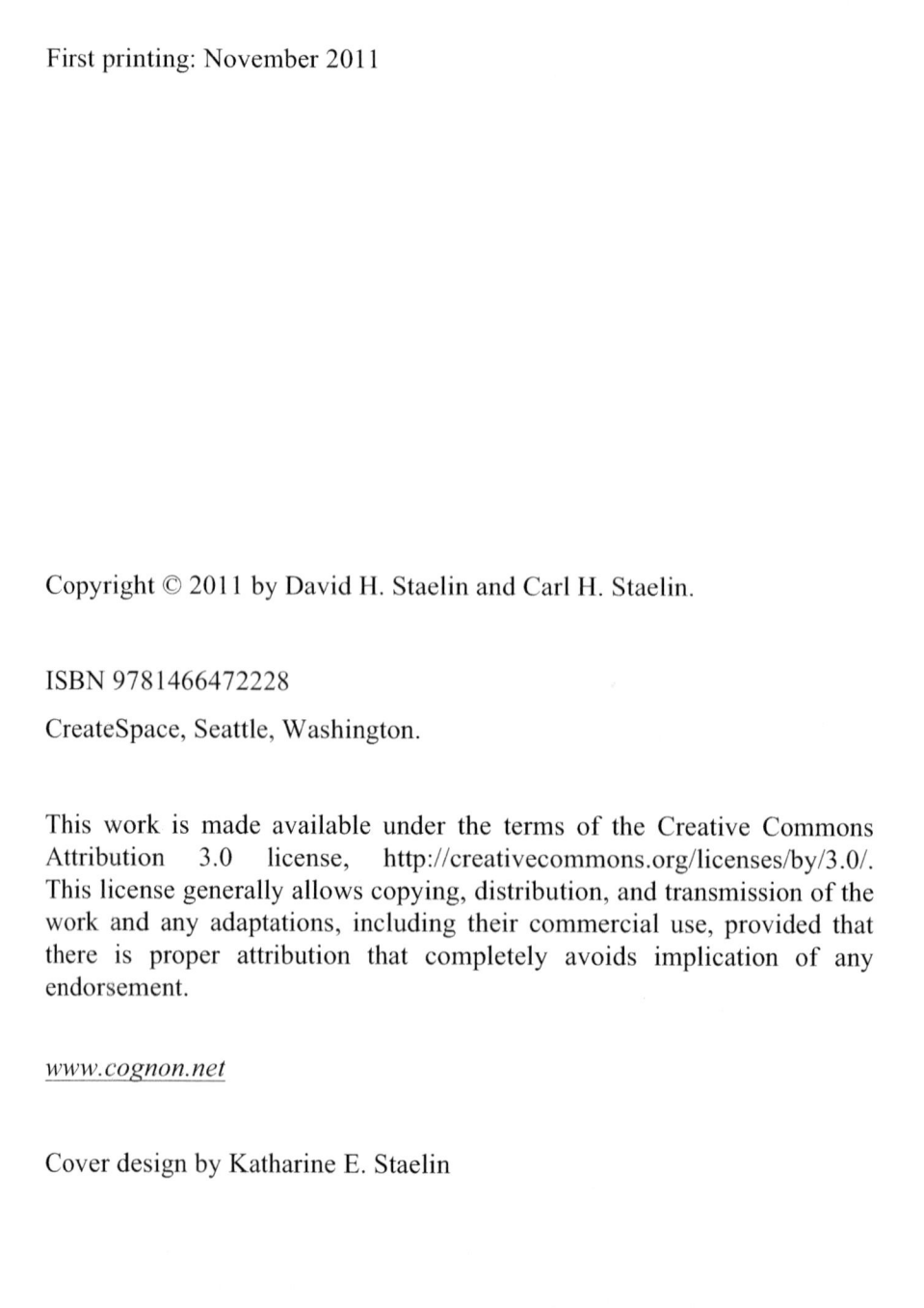

ISBN 9781466472228

CreateSpace, Seattle, Washington.

This work is made available under the terms of the Creative Commons Attribution 3.0 license, http://creativecommons.org/licenses/by/3.0/. This license generally allows copying, distribution, and transmission of the work and any adaptations, including their commercial use, provided that there is proper attribution that completely avoids implication of any endorsement.

www.cognon.net

Cover design by Katharine E. Staelin

Dedication

We dedicate this monograph to our wives and families who helped make this work possible and life worthwhile.

Abstract

This monograph addresses in a new way how brains may use signal spikes to compute, perceive, and support cognition. It presents and simulates simple novel numerical models of neurons and discusses the relationship between their performance and known neural behavior. Modest math skills combined with the included brief review of neural signaling should enable most readers to understand the basic issues while skimming over the more specialized portions. Readers more interested in perception and cognition might wish to begin with Chapter 1 and then jump to Section 5.3 and the rest of the text before returning to the beginning to read about the mathematics of spike processing.

Novel contributions include:

1) A simple binary neuron model (the "cognon model") that learns and recognizes complex spike excitation patterns in less than one second while requiring no unexpected neural properties or external training signals. An excitation pattern has no more than one spike per input synapse and typically lasts less than about 20 milliseconds.

2) A Shannon mutual information metric (recoverable bits/neuron) that assumes: 1) each neural spike indicates only that the responsible nearly simultaneous neuron input excitation pattern had probably been seen earlier while that neuron was "learning ready", and 2) the information is stored in synapse strengths. This focus on recallable learned information differs from most prior metrics such as pattern classification performance or those relying on specific training signals other than the normal input spikes.

3) Derivation of an equation for the Shannon metric that suggests such neurons can recall useful Shannon information only if their probability of firing randomly is lowered between learning and recall, where an increase in firing threshold before recall is one likely mechanism.

4) Extensions and analyses of cognon models that also use spike timing, dendrite compartments, and new learning mechanisms in addition to spike-timing-dependent plasticity (STDP).

5) Simulations that show how simple neuron models having between 200 and 10,000 binary-strength synapses can recall up to ~0.16 bits/synapse by optimizing various neuron and training parameters.

6) Translations of these simulation results into estimates for parameters like the average bits/spike, bits/neuron/second, maximum number of learnable patterns, optimum ratios between the strengths of weak and strong synapses, and probabilities of false alarms (output spikes triggered by unlearned patterns).

7) Concepts for how multiple layers of neurons can be trained sequentially in approximately linear time, even in the presence of rich feedback, and how such rich feedback might permit improved noise immunity, learning and recognition of pattern sequences, compression of data, associative or content-addressable memory, and development of communications links through white matter.

8) Report of a seemingly novel and rare human waking visual anomaly (WVA) that lasts less than a few seconds but seems consistent with these discussions of spike processing, rich feedback, and, surprisingly, video memories consistent with prior observations of accelerated time-reversed maze-running memories in sleeping rats.

9) Discussions of the possible relationship between the new neural spike feedback model and new experiments in the initiation and termination of transient weak hallucinations while the subjects were aware of their true surroundings. Some of these experiments may have useful medical implications.

Preface

Few grand challenges are more daunting than the intertwined mathematical, neurological, and cognitive mysteries of brain. This monograph addresses all three, but focuses primarily on the mathematical performance limits of neuron models that appear consistent with observations.

The most basic of these neuron models (the basic "cognon model") utilizes only two well-known properties of cortical neurons: 1) they produce a ~1-millisecond ~100-millivolt electrochemical output "spike" only when their synapse-weighted input spikes simultaneously sum to exceed a variable "firing threshold" for the instantaneous excitation pattern, and 2) the weight applied by each input terminal (the synapse strength) can increase long-term if it is excited when that neuron fired. In addition the only information conveyed by a cognon output spike is that the cognon was probably exposed to the responsible excitation pattern during a prior period of learning readiness.

Extensions of this basic cognon model allow precisely dispersed spike delays within a single pattern, multiple dendrite compartments, and alternative learning rules for synaptic strength. Because real neurons are far more complex they should perform better than cognons.

However, neuron model performance must be defined in a neurologically relevant way before it can be quantified and optimized. The Shannon information metric for the recallable taught information follows directly from our simplifying assumption that a spike implies only that a cognon's responsible current excitation pattern resembles one that it saw when it was "learning ready." This information metric (recallable bits/neuron) is simply the mutual information between the ensembles of taught and recalled patterns and depends on teaching strategy. It differs substantially from most prior information measures that do not restrict the metric to recallable learned information.

The ultimate test of this modeling strategy is whether or not these rudimentary neuron models can successfully recall large amounts of information when scaled up to reflect neurologically expected firing thresholds, numbers of synapses per neuron, spreads in synaptic strength, and spike frequencies. Our results of ~0.16 bits/synapse for cognons with up to 10,000 synapses rivals or exceeds most estimates obtained for other neuron models despite our minimalist and arguably plausible assumptions. Real neurons probably can perform even better since evolution has resulted in great neuron complexity involving many special purpose neurotransmitters and other components. This physical complexity presumably evolved to enable neurons and neural networks to utilize optimum signal processing techniques that we have yet to identify.

With this encouraging performance of ~0.16 bits/synapse we then extended the model to include substantial signal feedback and to show how feedback could arguably facilitate signal detection, storage, and content-addressable memory functions for both static and time-sequential patterns. This discussion then presents an apparently newly observed but very rare "waking visual anomaly" (WVA) that typically lasts less than a few seconds and seems consistent with the feedback model for spike processing. Most intriguing is WVA evidence that humans can recall movies played backward at high speed, as do some rats when dreaming of running mazes (Davidson, T., Kloosterman, F. & Wilson, M., 2009) Additional evidence from traditional hallucinations is also considered along with potential medical applications.

This monograph represents the product of the lead author's lifetime interest in brain function, supported by the second author's development and use of a series of spike-processing neural simulators. The hope of the authors is that the results and insights presented here will motivate and enable others to design new neuroscience experiments and to explore and extend these spike-processing neuron models at both the neuron and system level so as to improve understanding of brain function in ways that lead to useful medical and educational applications.

David H. Staelin and Carl H. Staelin

October 25, 2011

Table of Contents

1. Introduction
- 1.1. The challenge — 1
- 1.2. Brief review of basic neural structure — 5
- 1.3 Relevance of simple models to real neurons and networks — 10
- 1.4 Overview of monograph — 12

2. Basic model
- 2.1 Introduction — 14
- 2.2 Basic recognition neuron model — 15
- 2.3 Simulation results for the basic neural recognition model — 18
- 2.4 Probabilities of recognition and false alarm — 21
- 2.5 Recognition by layered spike-processing neural models — 28
- 2.6 Basic spike-processing neural learning model — 30
- 2.7 Shannon information metric — 33
- 2.8 Simulations of the cognon basic (CB) learning model — 36
- 2.9 Summary and next steps — 41

3. Full neural model
- 3.1 Extensions of the cognon neural model — 44
- 3.2 Issues in derivation of the information stored per neuron — 48
- 3.3 Simulations of the cognon extended (CE) model — 52
- 3.4 Extended cognon time-domain simulator — 67

4. Relationship between neuron models and neuroscience
- 4.1 Summary of the key results of Chapters 2 and 3 — 71
- 4.2 Initial training of multi-layer neural systems — 72

5. Spike computations, feedback, and cognition
- 5.1 Training of feedback paths using spikes — 77
- 5.2 Uses for strong spike-based feedback — 79
- 5.3 Cognition with spikes — 81
- 5.4 Inter-regional training and communication via white matter — 87
- 5.5 Approaches to analyzing neural networks with rich feedback — 90

6. Waking visual anomalies, hallucinations, and cognons
- 6.1 Observations and interpretations of waking visual anomalies — 92
- 6.2 Experiments in initiating and terminating hallucinations — 101

7. Summary and conclusions — 107

Table of Contents – continued

Appendix A. Derivation of L, the information stored per neuron   109

Appendix B. Basic and extended neuron simulator description   113

References   126

Acknowledgements   130

About the Authors   131

Chapter 1
Introduction

1.1 The challenge

Understanding how the human brain computes so rapidly using neural spikes remains a challenging intellectual problem. This monograph uses simple neural models to show how spike-based processing can support rapid learning and recognition of complex patterns, and how certain mathematical considerations may limit the brain's computational performance as a function of neuron architecture.

Readers more interested in perception and cognition might wish to begin with this Chapter and then jump to Section 5.3 and the rest of the text, where perception and cognition are discussed more generally, before returning to the beginning to read about the mathematics of spike processing that enables such perception and cognition.

Neurons are the basic computational units of the brain and perform both logic and wiring functions as single interconnected cells. Simulations show that the new model neurons presented here (called cognons) can learn a single complex excitation pattern in less than a second, and can each neuron learn to recognize hundreds of distinct patterns in a manner arguably consistent with known neural behavior.

General considerations then suggest how significant feedback of spikes from upper neural layers might facilitate recognition of noisy, time-sequential, or partial patterns. This leads to a discussion of how transient flaws in the same feedback mechanisms can yield informative phenomena, as supported by experiments involving initiation and termination of mild visual, auditory, and olfactory illusions.

The presentation is intended to be largely accessible to broad audiences, from scientists and engineers to interested technically minded lay people. A brief review of basic neuroscience is provided for those new to the field, and the significance of most mathematical and less accessible elements is summarized in more understandable terms throughout the text. It is hoped that most readers encountering difficult sections will generally be able to skip over them while retaining the essence of the presentation.

Observations of the brain show that neural signals consist mostly of spikes of perhaps one-millisecond duration, or bursts of such spikes. We ignore here the special case of rapid bursts. Although voltage pulses traveling along single or bundled metal wires have long been studied and utilized by computer and communications engineers, most such wires have only one or a few destinations. In strong contrast, a spike from a typical neuron might stimulate 10,000 other neurons, each of which might then feed 10,000 others. Such architectures have no obvious counterparts within traditional communications or computer science.

Moreover, simultaneous observation of all inputs and outputs from even a single typical neuron having thousands of connections is so difficult that its exact mathematical operation must be inferred from partial data, and the situation becomes even more problematic when networks of such highly interconnected neurons are probed. This elusiveness of the computational issues contrasts strongly with the enormous amount already known about the brain's biochemistry, structure, and connections because of the much more powerful observational tools available for such physical studies.

Another strong difference between neurons and logic elements is that neurons produce a spike primarily when their inputs are excited with more than some threshold number of spikes within one or a few milliseconds, where the threshold might be ten or more simultaneous spikes, and a typical neuron might produce only a few output spikes per second. In contrast, the building blocks of most computer, communications, and algorithmic systems involve simple logic gates or operators that respond to no more than a few simultaneous inputs on the same few wires, and then excite only a few other such elements at roughly gigahertz rates (10^9 per second).

The very slow rate of brain signaling by single neurons is therefore compensated by its vastly greater parallelism and interconnectivity, where a human brain might employ $10^{11} - 10^{12}$ neurons. Modern computers (e.g., CPU's in 2011) appear to approach the human brain when one multiplies three numbers: the number of register bits (say 10^3 for computers and 10^{11} neurons for brain) times the average operations per second of each (say ~10^{10} for computers and ~4 for brain) times the average number of active outputs per element (say ~4 for computers and ~10^4 for brain); these products are then 4×10^{13} for computers and 4×10^{15} for the brain. A brain with 10^{14} synapses that each store an average of 0.1 bit is roughly equivalent to a 1-terabyte computer memory. Since there are many things that computers and brains can do that the other cannot, this hybrid computational metric (the product of three numbers) is only suggestive at best.

One result of these differences relative to computer and communications science is that there is little prior art useful for understanding the computational basis of brain. For example, the best current real-time observations of neural spikes monitor only a few hundred outputs, mostly from different neurons. Unfortunately there are no simultaneous observations of all 10,000 inputs to a single neuron, or even a majority of them, nor are such observations likely soon because of their difficulty. Part of the difficulty is that such multi-neuron probes sample sets of neurons that are determined by where the probes randomly land within the neural tissue. Targeting is difficult because neuron cell bodies have diameters on the order of 50 microns while the intensely intertwined "wires", dendrites and axons, have diameters on the order of 1 and 0.2 microns, respectively. As a result the exact computational function of neurons must be inferred from complex indirect experiments providing incomplete information, and much remains unknown.

This monograph focuses instead more on the mathematical properties and limitations of various alternative neural computational models with the hope that they could arguably support perception while also being consistent with existing neurological observations. As mentioned earlier, the models studied here will be arguably shown to have this potential, although much remains to be learned. The greater complexity of real neurons could only improve the performance of the simple models because, in a mathematical sense, simple models are a small subset of all possible models.

Some existing neurological observations are sufficiently demanding that they preclude most alternative models. Foremost among these observations are that: 1) humans can learn new complex visual and auditory patterns in less than one second and recognize them thereafter, also within less than a second, 2) this rapid learning and recall is based on typical spike separations of tens of milliseconds within attentive neurons, which implies that a maximum of a few spikes are required per participating neuron per recognition event, and 3) the information content of the DNA that defines the brain (conservatively fewer than 10^{10} bits) is far less than the information content of an educated brain (conservatively more than 10^{12} bits); this implies that most information is not innate but must be learned by deep networks of neurons that appear locally to be wired randomly.

In addition to constraints imposed by observations there is an important constraint imposed by computer theory. That is, early models for neural learning often assumed that neurons and synapses learned by being "rewarded" when a "trainer" of unspecified origin determined that the neuron had responded correctly to a given input excitation pattern, and that it was "punished" when it responded incorrectly. This paradigm is closely related to the back-propagation training protocols widely used in multi-layer artificial neural networks (ANN) designed for various practical signal processing tasks. ANN originally used analog signals rather than spike timing under the assumption that neural information was more likely conveyed by spike frequency; now analog signals are used because they are so useful in practice. ANN training is a slow iterative process that does not match observed behavior of instant learning.

The strengths of ANN synapses connecting an output neuron to one or more input neurons are individually increased or decreased depending on the degree to which they contributed to each desired output strength of the second neuron as determined by a "trainer" that both provides the training inputs to the first neural layer and the desired output of the output neuron. At least two ANN layers are typically involved, and often more.

However, it has been shown that training of synapses that link as few as two ANN neurons located in one neural layer to one neuron in the next layer is impossibly slow relative to the nearly instant learning capabilities of humans (Blum & Rivest, 1992). This is because inter-neuron back-propagation training times are arguably NP-complete in the number of connections per neuron. This suggests that neural training times are exponential in the number of inter-neural connections, which might approximate 10,000. The implication is that instant learning must be implemented by intra-neural (single neuron) training rather than by inter-neural training. Unfortunately, few other useful mathematical constraints on neural learning have been developed.

This shortage of prior art motivates beginning with simplified neural models that roughly approximate known neural behavior while also permitting mathematical analysis of their learning and recall performance. Our original hope was that the simplest neural model that is arguably consistent with most basic physical properties of neurons would also arguably rival observed neural computational performance. We were optimistic that simple models might suffice because cortical architecture is similar across a single cortex despite the very different visual, auditory, olfactory, tactile, motor, and other functions performed by its various regions.

Cortex is the gently wrinkled layer of computational grey matter perhaps 1-2 mm thick that wraps around the white matter that wires the various cortical regions together. Since cortical architecture is similar across most animal species it seems plausible that cortex may have evolved to optimize universal mathematical performance limits within biological constraints. This optimism concerning the potentially high computational performance of simple neuron models was ultimately justified by the cognon simulations presented later.

1.2 Brief review of neural structure

The brain consists mostly of "gray matter" and "white matter," where most gray matter resides in an outer cortical layer about 1-2 mm thick folded in a convoluted way around the white matter which rapidly propagates signals from one region of the brain to another. Gray matter is roughly analogous to the logic circuits of computers, while white matter is more analogous to wires having limited logic functionality.

Typical neurons in cortex resemble trees perhaps 0.2 – 1 mm in height, although their forms vary widely. The "roots" where neural input signals arrive are called dendrites, the "stubby trunk" where the spikes are generated is called the cell body or soma, and the thin "branches" along which the output spikes travel are called axons. These components are suggested in Figure 1.1. Full arrays of axons and dendrites associated with a neuron are sometimes called axon and dendrite arbors, respectively, because of their tree-like forms. The junction between one axon branch (output) of one neuron and a dendrite (input) of another occurs at a synapse, and the number of potential inputs per neuron equals its number of afferent (input) synapses, which can be 10,000 or more (Braitenberg & Schuz; 1999, Koch, 1999).

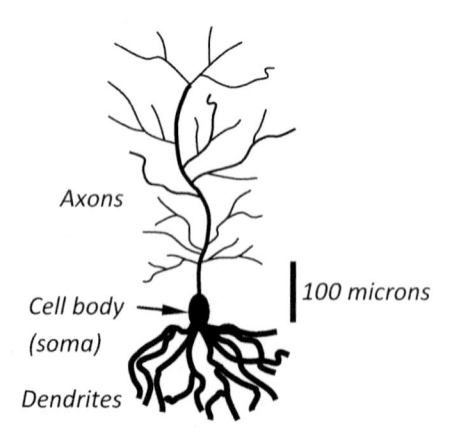

Figure 1.1 Artist's sketch of a typical neuron with its dendrite arbor below, the soma or cell body in the center, and the axon arbor above.

Because axons continually add sufficient energy to their propagating spikes to compensate for any attenuation, the spikes arrive at the tip of each axon branch with comparable energy and duration. A spike is an electrochemical phenomenon of roughly 1-millivolt amplitude that propagates along cortical axons and dendrites at speeds that vary between many meters per second in large axons down to fractions of a meter per second in the thinnest axons having diameters approaching 0.1 micron. It has been suggested that a single cubic millimeter of cortex might contain up to 4 km of axons (wires), orders of magnitude beyond anything yet achieved by industry.

The strength of each synapse varies individually with learning — it is the prime locus of memory, in combination with the identities of the two neurons it links. Most basic neuron models assume that they spike when the nearly simultaneous sum of their input spikes weighted by their respective synapse strengths exceeds some firing threshold H that varies with time (McCulloch & Pitts, 1943; Koch, 1999; VanRullen, Guyonneau, & Thorpe, 2005). In our simplified binary models of neurons we assume all spikes have the same amplitude and shape, while synapses have only two possible strengths, 1 and G ($G > 1$), where the option of $G = 0$ is treated separately later.

Since this threshold model is so central, it bears repeating. A basic threshold-firing neuron model produces an output spike only if during a 1-millisecond period, say, the summed excitation at that neuron's dendrites exceeded the neuron's firing threshold. The summed excitation is the sum of each input spike arriving during that same period, weighted by the strength of each corresponding input synapse. For example, if during a single pattern period 20 excitation spikes arrived at 20 strong synapses each of strength G, then the sum would be $20G$. If the firing threshold were $20G$, the neuron would instantly fire and produce an output spike that would propagate quickly and unattenuated to the tip of each output axon branch to excite perhaps 10,000 other neurons. If the same 20 excitation spikes happened to arrive instead at 20 weak synapses, each having strength of 1, then the sum would be only 20, which would be below the firing threshold $20G$ ($G > 1$) and no output spike would be generated.

Thus, within the nominal 1-millisecond period, only arriving input spike patterns that almost exclusively excite strong synapses would cause the neuron to fire, and it is these patterns that the neuron would recognize. Training of such a neuron consists of strengthening the sparse set of synapses that best corresponds to all the patterns that the neuron should recognize, and all useful stored information subsequently resides in that pattern of synapse strengths.

Although many synapses in nature have negative strengths or are otherwise inhibitory (perhaps 10 percent of them), they apparently are not essential based on the high performance of our simulated models that have only non-negative binary synapse strengths. Thus a weak positive synapse is not very different in a mathematical sense from a positively biased negative synapse since biases can be corrected by adjusting the neuron firing threshold. Inhibitory synapses undoubtedly improve neuron performance in unknown ways, perhaps by counteracting over generalizations during pattern recognition, or by improving system efficiency.

We assume that the basic unit of input information processed by a single neuron is a binary pattern of nearly simultaneous excitation spikes; each input is either a spike or not, in each nominal 1-millisecond period. In the simplest case all spikes in a single excitation pattern arrive nearly simultaneously at the neuron cell body of interest. We explore later more complex models that also respond to small time offsets, typically less than 10-20 milliseconds, between spikes within a single excitation pattern. Modest pattern time separations greater than approximately 20 milliseconds are then assumed to distinguish one excitation pattern from another. We ignore neural models that learn and respond to time intervals between the successive arrival times of spikes at individual synapses. This is because the mechanism is unclear and adequate neuron model performance is being obtained using a simpler model. Nonetheless, that signaling modality may sometimes be utilized.

The well-known brain-wave frequencies observed by EEG scalp recordings are plausible evidence of periodic pattern presentations, where different frequency bands may be associated with different cognitive functions or regions of the brain. One band of interest is the ~40-Hz gamma band that is often active when animals are attentive to their surroundings (Steinmetz et al., 2000). This response might correspond to successive pattern presentations at ~25-msec intervals. The spikes composing such patterns might be synchronized by mechanisms such as visual saccades (Gollisch & Meister, 2008) or the passage of most inter-regional neurons through the thalamus, a part of the brain known to have a timing function. Synchronization mechanisms for either patterns or spikes are not yet well understood.

All physical systems exhibit noise, and neural noise usually manifests as isolated spontaneous spikes, random fluctuations of the firing threshold, or random variations of spike amplitudes or arrival times prior to summation. Since output spikes indicate pattern detection, any spontaneously emitted but meaningless output spikes are "false alarms" that limit the information that can be extracted from neurons, and spikes not generated during recall because of mistiming or inadequate amplitudes constitute missed detections. These baseline false alarm and missed detection rates partially control memory performance.

Before birth the neurons start to multiply and take their assigned places within the brain, where their structural details then adapt to the local task. Most wiring that connects neurons appears visually to be random and somewhat dynamic. New connections between neurons are continually being formed, particularly during youth, and these synaptic connections typically eventually atrophy so that the net number of connections in the brain changes only slowly, reaching a peak in midlife. New neurons also continually form and atrophy, as do synapses, but on a much slower and perhaps decadal time scale.

At the system level the brain is divided into functional regions that perform visual, auditory, tactile, somatic (smell), motor, memory, and other functions; some regional boundaries are visible upon dissection and some are not. Although both cortical neuron characteristics and their connection patterns vary from region to region, most cortex has six visibly defined layers of physically differentiated neurons within its ~2-mm thickness where this structure exhibits relatively few visible differences across all cortex. Generally the lower neural levels perform operations that are more at the pixel and feature level and are often localized in space, time, or frequency, while higher levels recognize more complex and less local objects and concepts (Freiwald & Tsao, 2010). Additional features of neural networks are explained when they are introduced.

1.3 Relevance of simple models to real neurons and networks

The contributions of numerical models to neuroscience and to understanding the limits of the abilities of real neurons to compute and communicate have unfortunately been limited, placing this approach at a perceived disadvantage despite its potential.

For example, many neuroscientists ask how simplified numerical models of neurons and neural networks could contribute useful understanding since they differ so markedly from real neurons. One answer to this important question is that if the behavior of simple numerical models is a subset of the achievable complex behaviors of real neurons then such model studies can establish an approximate lower bound to real performance. If that lower-bound performance is good, such models can be illuminating and may suggest new questions for experimental or theoretical study. The dependence of the performance of "good" neural models upon neural parameters can also be illuminating, as discussed later.

Unfortunately, we know of no neural models prior to those presented here that are arguably consistent with both observed neural behavior and sub-second learning and recall. For example, many fast-learning models invoke training signals of unknown origin. It is important to note that modulation of "learning readiness" is not a training signal for teaching specific excitation patterns or classification rules. Learning readiness simply enables large groups of neurons to learn whatever excitation patterns they see when the animal is in an alert or excited state.

The basic cognon model presented later assumes only that a neuron spikes when the sum of its concurrent inputs exceeds a threshold, and that if a neuron is learning ready, then an output spike can modestly strengthen those synapses that contributed to that spike; both these general neural properties are well known and are discussed later (Koch, 1999). As simulations will show, our basic-model performance levels can be quite high with few obvious requirements for further improvement in metrics such as bits/neuron, bits/synapse, bits/neuron/second, learning and recall speeds, etc.

Another concern of many scientists is that new models should be carefully linked to their predecessors so that the historic flow of the field is evident and the reasons for different conclusions become apparent. This is a reasonable desire and is the existing paradigm within physical neuroscience, but if a new numerical model is promising and well defended by simple repeatable experiments, then relating it to extensive prior art based on fundamentally different assumptions can be a counter-productive diversion. This is the view taken here, and references to such work are provided instead of reviews.

This issue of prior art particularly arises with respect to the information theory metric chosen later. The choice made here is the unique Shannon metric (Shannon, 1948) that applies when: 1) the desired information is the "taught" information that can be recovered by observing the model's outputs for all possible input excitation patterns, and 2) the only information provided by a neural spike is that the excitation pattern responsible for that spike had excited approximately the same synapses that had been strengthened earlier as a result of seeing similar excitation patterns when the synapses were plastic and learning-ready. No other learned-information storage and recovery mechanism is assumed for the basic neuron model offered here.

In contrast, the prior art often assumes another information transfer process or metric is involved that may include information residing in the time interval between two consecutive spikes or perhaps some information unrelated to the recallable learned information. For example, many such papers evaluate Shannon information and rate distortion metrics based on the observed and modeled joint probability distributions of the inputs and outputs of mature neurons rather than on the success of the learning and recall process, which is a key metric in our study (Berger, 2003; Averbeck, Latham, & Pouget, 2006; Quiroga & Panzeri, 2009; Linsker, 1989; Parra, Beck, & Bell, 2009; Coleman & Sarma, 2010; Buesing & Maass, 2010).

Finally, there is the question of the utility of linking simple numerical models to non-repeatable natural experiments such as the novel waking visual anomalies (WVA) reported here (WVA last less than a few seconds when normal healthy subjects awake and are extremely rare) and to various properties of hallucinations. The utility of WVA was arguably demonstrated by its inspiration of our study of neural models using intra-pattern spike timing to boost neural performance, and by the WVA evidence discussed in Section 6.1 that humans may also exhibit high-speed reverse-time recall of visual memories, just as do some sleeping rats recalling maze-running experiences (Davidson, Kloosterman, & Wilson, 2009). The utility of relating these models to mild hallucinations in Section 6.2 is their arguable consistency plus the fact that the models suggest palliative remedies that appear effective in some cases.

1.4 Overview of monograph

To facilitate readability, the more discipline-specific details are postponed to later chapters. Chapter 2 presents the simple basic neuron model, which is broadly consistent with the minimum assumptions made by most other authors. Initially only the recognition mechanism of the basic neuron model is presented and simulated in Section 2.2, followed by presentation and time-domain simulation of one possible neuron training model in Section 2.3. Section 2.4 derives and discusses the probability of learning and false alarm. Section 2.5 describes how multilayer neural networks might recognize patterns, while Section 2.6 discusses how it might learn. Section 2.7 introduces Shannon information theory to facilitate understanding of the mathematical performance bounds of such models, but postpones more complete discussion to Chapter 3.

Chapter 3 then extends the basic model by introducing the optional possibilities that: 1) neuron firing decisions might be performed within dendritic sectors (compartments) that independently sum their own synapse excitations and test that sum against their own firing threshold before firing the neuron, and 2) the relative timing of spikes within a single neuron excitation pattern (which might last 2-20 milliseconds) could further distinguish one pattern from another. An additional learning model involving synapse atrophy is also introduced along with a derivation of the information theory metric used to compare the performance of the various neural models. Each model is then simulated and the resulting relationships between the neuron model parameters and neuron performance are tabulated and converted to approximate polynomials. These polynomials suggest why optimum values of parameters such as the firing threshold and firing rate might depend on the primary purpose of the neuron.

Chapter 4 links these results to the observed form and behavior of cortical neurons, although they vary so much that these links are only suggestive. Chapters 5 and 6 are less quantitative and more speculative. Chapter 5 suggests how these neural models and network architectures might help explain cognition, and Chapter 6 explores in a limited way the potential utility of recently observed waking visual anomalies (WVA) for revealing additional information about cortical architecture and signaling. It also discusses experiments involving the initiation and termination of brief hallucinations that appear consistent with the qualitative discussion in Chapter 5 concerning cognition and that suggest possible clinical applications. Chapter 7 then concludes with suggestions for future work.

Chapter 2
Basic model

2.1 Introduction

This chapter first postulates in Section 2.2 and then simulates in Section 2.3 the recognition performance of the simplest neurologically plausible single-neuron model that appears capable of learning novel input patterns instantly and later signaling each subsequent re-appearance with a recognition spike while largely ignoring most unlearned patterns. Section 2.4 presents some simple theoretical performance equations, and Section 2.5 briefly discusses how single-neuron recognition performance could enable recognition of more complex patterns by large networks of such neurons.

Section 2.6 then adds a learning mechanism to this basic recognition model and defines the "cognon" family of neuron models. Section 2.7 defines a metric for the average Shannon information (bits/neuron) retrievable from a trained basic learning neuron, and Section 2.8 simulates its learning and recall performance. It is shown that single neurons can produce output spikes in response to their input excitation patterns with low probabilities of error if they were exposed to those same patterns during prior sub-second learning periods. The probability of responding to untrained patterns during recall can be made almost arbitrarily small, although at the expense of the total number of patterns that can be learned. This section then maximizes the Shannon information by optimizing certain learning parameters for various neuron models. Extensions to these basic models presented in Chapter 3 yield still further performance improvements.

2.2 Basic recognition neuron model

The basic recognition neuron model uses a well-known property of neurons: they "fire" by producing an output spike only when the sum of simultaneous (within a few milliseconds) identical input spikes weighted by each synapse strength exceeds some firing threshold, where the set of simultaneously excited neural inputs defines the neuron input "pattern." The patterns recognizable by a neuron are therefore determined by that neuron's input (afferent) synaptic weights.

This basic model is further simplified by assuming that all spikes have the same amplitude and time of arrival within a given excitation pattern, and that the binary synaptic weights exhibit only one of two possible values, say 1 and $G > 1$, without significant loss of generality. Since the input patterns must be sparse in order to achieve selective pattern recognition performance, the number of simultaneously excited input spikes must be quite small compared to S_o, the number of synapses per neuron. In nature, fewer than one-tenth of a neuron's inputs are typically excited simultaneously.

The architecture of our basic neural model and the definition of its excitation pattern are explained in Figure 2.1, which illustrates a single-neuron computational model. It is important to note that this model has many inputs and only one output, each terminal being a neuron soma that may spike; thus it includes the axons of the input neurons but excludes the axons of the output neuron. This shift away from a pure single neuron definition simplifies definition of our performance metric and the subsequent computations because there is only one output. This model definition becomes particularly important when variable axon propagation delays can alter the input excitation delay pattern before spike summation by the neuron, as is explored in Chapter 3.

Each excitation pattern is a sequence of 0's and 1's that correspond respectively to the absence or presence of a spike at the afferent soma (input neurons) within the same nominal millisecond window during which spikes can superimpose efficiently. The pattern is not the input to the synapses, which could differ if the paths between the various afferent soma and the summing point introduce additional different fixed delays, as is

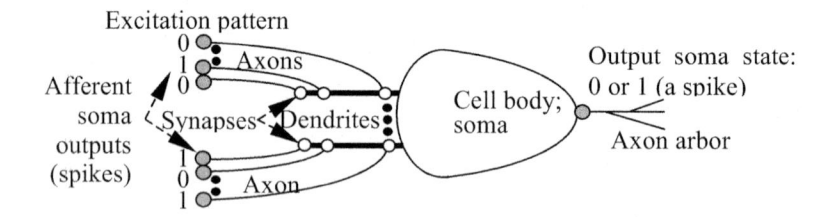

Figure 2.1. Neural model architecture and soma-based definition of excitation patterns.

permitted in Chapter 3. The output (zero or one) is defined by whether the neuron produces a nearly simultaneous spike at the neuron output (right-hand side of the figure), where each output spike signifies recognition of the input as familiar.

Each neuron output spike propagates along a highly branched axon "arbor" that might extend to ~0.5 mm length or more. Each small axon branch typically terminates in a synapse that connects to a dendrite on another neuron. Dendrites are generally shorter and thicker than axons and connect to the cell body and "soma" where the basic neuron model sums the excitations over a sliding time window that we approximate using discrete time intervals of ~1 millisecond width (say). If the sum equals or exceeds the firing threshold, then the basic neuron model fires. In nature, patterns might be presented at intervals of tens of milliseconds, and perhaps at the well-known gamma, theta, or other periodicities of brain.

Figure 2.2 suggests the detection performance of a single basic neuron model for the very simple case where each input pattern always excites exactly $N = 4$ input neurons; this leads to simple mathematical estimates for the probabilities of detection and false alarm, where a false alarm results whenever an unlearned pattern produces a recognition output spike. The horizontal axis represents the time at which each excitation pattern might be presented for recognition, nominally within one-millisecond windows spaced perhaps 25 milliseconds apart, which would be consistent with EEG gamma waves.

The first two patterns, A and B, correspond to the two patterns this model learned to recognize earlier; learning is discussed later. The black

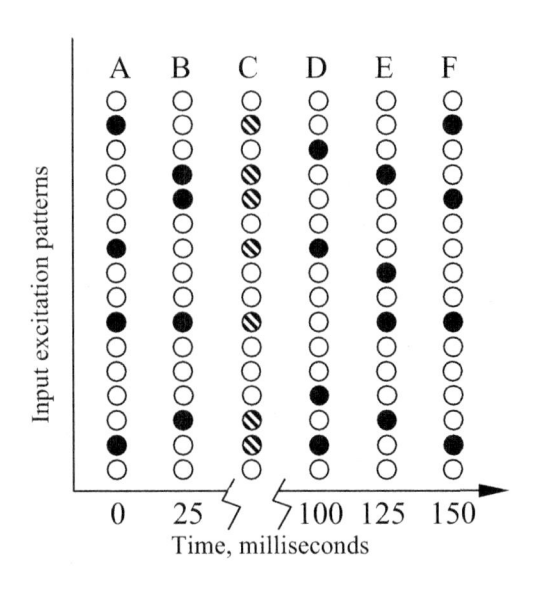

Figure 2.2. Examples of learned excitation patterns (A and B, black circles), synapses with strengthened gains G (crosshatched) and initial gains of unity (open circles), and test input excitation patterns (D-F, black circles) that reveal whether the neuron would spike when excited with those inputs during a recognition test. Each excitation pattern here has 16 input neurons driving a different subset of 16 synapses of the basic recognition model every 25 milliseconds. Patterns D, E, and F produce excitation sums of 2, 3, and 4, respectively, where only F causes a false alarm because the firing threshold equals four.

dots indicate which input neurons fired for that pattern, and the open dots correspond to those that did not fire. The third vector, C, indicates which corresponding synapses have strength $G > 1$ (gray circles) when recall is tested, whereas the rest have unity strength. The next three random vectors (D, E, F) with $N = 4$ excited inputs (black circles) were not in the learned set and, except for pattern F, do not produce an output recognition spike; F produces a false alarm because it fires but was not taught.

Although it is apparent from Figure 2.2 that if S_o were to be increased to thousands ($S_o = 16$ here), and if N were to remain in the 4-60 range, many patterns sparsely populated with "one's" could be reliably recognized by a single neuron with low false-alarm probabilities. This is particularly so when any contributions from weak untrained synapses during recognition are negligible because the ratio of trained to untrained synapse strengths is the gain $G \gg 1$ during recall when patterns are being recognized.

The number of patterns that can be taught is limited by the risk of false alarms, which are reduced if the w learned patterns share an above-average number of synapses, thereby minimizing the total number S_G of strong synapses. Initially S_G is zero. If the taught patterns are random then S_G increases more rapidly with w, and the case where no two learned patterns utilize the same synapses is worse. For example, in the worst case no more than $w \cong S_o/3N$ patterns can be safely learned, assuming $S_o \cong 3S_G$ is safe. This conservative limit suggests that when $N = 40$ and $S_o = 12,000$, then $w < \sim 100$ learned patterns; in practice the limit for w would be higher for random patterns, and still higher if the taught patterns shared an above-average number of synapses in common while remaining distinct.

2.3 Simulation results for the basic neural recognition model

Table 2.1 presents the average false-alarm probabilities p_F that result for various assumed model parameters using the basic recognition neuron model described in Section 2.2 and the corresponding model simulator described in Section 2.9 and Appendix B. In every case the conservatively listed p_F equals the estimated p_F plus its estimated standard deviation based on numerous independent simulations. In cases where the estimated rms accuracy of p_F is more than half the estimated value for p_F, its entry is flagged with (*). Discussion concerning the listed variable L (bits, recoverable learned information) is postponed until Section 2.8.

The low values for p_F near 1 percent suggest that in these cases the basic learning neuron model should emit no more than one spontaneous erroneous spike every hundred patterns or so, or perhaps one every three seconds if 30 different random novel patterns are presented for recognition per second. The high sensitivity of p_F to both N and w is indicated by the effects of changing $N = 4$ to $N = 5$ in the second row of the table, and w from 1 to 2 in the third row. This extreme sensitivity of p_F also contributes to its sometimes relatively large standard variation when estimated using finite simulations.

Table 2.1. False alarm recognition probabilities p_F as a function of the basic recognition model neuron parameters

p_F(%)	N	H	S_o	w	G	L	L/S_o
0.00	4	4	10	1	100	8.5	0.85
10.9	5	4	10	1	100	3.3	0.33
18.9*	4	4	10	2	100	7.1	0.70
0.00	10	10	100	4	100	34	0.34
0.06*	11	10	100	4	100	34	0.34
0.25*	11	10	100	5	100	40	0.40
0.54	11	10	1000	60	100	429	0.43
0.46	11	10	10,000	600	100	4296	0.43
0.38	22	20	10,000	450	100	3296	0.33
0.09*	10	10	100	6	1.5	50	0.50
0.02*	11	10	1000	15	1.5	127	0.10
0.01*	11	10	10,000	160	1.5	1354	0.13
1.95	14	10	10,000	10	1.5	58	0.01

Abbreviations: p_F = false-alarm probability, N = # of excited inputs, H = firing threshold, S_o = # of synapses, w = # patterns presented for learning, G = ratio of strong to weak synapses, L = recallable information.
* Estimated rms accuracy of p_F exceeds half the estimated value for p_F

The value of p_F can be made almost arbitrarily small for the larger neurons having $S_o > 100$ simply by reducing w so that very few synapses are strengthened. In the limit where $N = H$ and $w = 1$ the false alarm probability p_F is zero while the probability of recognition for that one pattern is unity. p_F can also be reduced by increasing G, but once N/G becomes less than unity a worst-case set of N excited weak synapses cannot increase the weighted sum excitation by even one unit, and therefore cannot cause false firing and change the outcome.

The main result evident from Table 2.1 is therefore that the basic recognition neuron model can instantly recognize even hundreds of patterns with little error. This is also true of the early Willshaw model (Willshaw, Buneman, & Longuet-Higgins, 1969; Graham & Willshaw, 1999) and a few others, so instant recognition alone is not unique to our model. The uniqueness lies instead in the relative neurological plausibility of the fast learning mechanism proposed for training our basic recognition neural model, as discussed in Sections 2.6 and 2.8.

The entries in Table 2.1 are more accurate that the theoretical approximations derived later in Section 2.4, which suggest the underlying mathematical issues. The details of the simulations are described briefly in Section 2.9 and in more detail in Appendix B. The main assumption was that the neuron fires only if the sum of the weighted excitations for both strong and weak synapses equals or exceeds the firing threshold $G \cdot H$:

$$G \cdot N_G + N - N_G \geq G \cdot H \tag{2.1}$$

where $G \cdot H$ is the firing threshold during recognition, N_G is the number of excited inputs that align with the strengthened synapses having $G > 1$, and $N - N_G$ is the number of other excited inputs that align with synapses having $G = 1$. In the limit where $GN_G \gg N - N_G$, the neuron fires simply if the number N_G of excited synapses with $G > 1$ exceeds the firing threshold H. For cases in Table 2.1 where $G = 100$ this is always the case.

Earlier we defined N as the number of excited input neurons for a given excitation pattern, S_o as the number of afferent synapses for the basic recognition model neuron, G as the greater of the two possible synapse strengths, unity being the other, and $G \cdot H$ as the assumed firing threshold during recognition. H is the lower firing threshold assumed for one basic learning model discussed later, and w is the number of patterns that the neuron model was trained to recognize.

The top part of Table 2.1 shows how both N and w are limited by the acceptable false alarm probability p_F, and how larger neurons (larger S_o) can store many patterns before failing due to an excessive number of learned patterns w, which is equivalent to "over education."

The lower part of Table 2.1 suggests that p_F can remain low even when the synapse strength varies by only a factor of $G = 1.5$ between those synapses that characterize the pattern to be recognized and those that do not. Such smaller values of G are roughly consistent with observed synaptic strength changes induced by learning, as discussed further in Section 2.6.

2.4 Probabilities of recognition and false alarm

It is useful to estimate the numerical probabilities of recognition p_L and false alarm p_F for given input patterns because the resulting equations provide some insight into the issues involved. $p_L = p_F$ during learning readiness because any random pattern that fires is immediately learned. These two probabilities are also key parameters needed later to compute the information L (bits) recallable by a single neuron. For convenience as we continue, Table 2.2 summarizes the definitions of symbols used in Chapter 2.

Table 2.2. Symbols used in Chapter 2

Symbol	Brief Definition
G	Ratio of strong synapse strength to weak synapse strength, binary approximation
H	Number of synapses needed to fire a neuron
I	Shannon information metric
L	Recallable learned Shannon information; here, the mutual information $I(X,Y)$
M	Number of neurons in a given neural network
N	Number of excited synapses at the neural model input
N'	Mean number of strengthened synapses in a neuron trained to recognize w patterns
p_F	False alarm probability for a random excitation pattern
p_i	Probability of message i being sent during a communication
p_L	Probability that a given taught pattern will be learned by a neuron
R	Average number of different patterns presented before a given neuron fires
S_G	Number of synapses on a single neuron that have strength G
S_o	Number of synapses on a single neuron of either strength
w	Number of patterns taught while a neuron model is learning ready (not all taught patterns are learned)

Assume first that the only pattern the neuron has learned has N spiking input neurons out of the set of S_o, and that all these excited input neurons feed those N synapses that have strength $G > 1$. If the firing threshold is $N \cdot G$ then the basic neuron model will always fire when a previously learned pattern is presented. If all patterns excite exactly N synapses, then to avoid false alarms for a one-pattern neuron we merely need a firing threshold $N \cdot G$ during recall that is sufficiently high that no other pattern can fire the neuron; for this special case it is sufficient that $G = 1 + \delta$, $\delta > 0$. p_F remains small even if the excitation pattern contains more than N excited inputs since the only patterns that will trigger a false alarm must excite all the synapses utilized by the one memorized pattern, provided that G is sufficiently large that all excitations of weak synapses add negligibly to the sum.

As the number N of excited synapses exceeds the number H of excited synapses needed to fire, and as G declines toward unity, the unity-strength synapses contribute more to the excitation sum tested against the firing threshold $G \cdot H$ and the false alarm probability p_F slowly increases. Numerical expressions for the exact detection and false-alarm probabilities can readily be derived for these cases but are not much more illuminating than the approximate expressions presented here and the simulation results presented in Section 2.8.

The false alarm probability p_F also slowly increases as the number w of patterns taught increases, where we temporarily assume all taught patterns were learned. We again simplify the math by assuming $N = H$. First we note that if $w = 1$, the probability that a given synapse in a set of S_o has strength $G = 1$ is simply $(S_o - N)/S_o$. If $w > 1$, this probability becomes $[(S_o - N)/S_o]^w$. If we further assume all learned patterns are independent, then the mean number of weak synapses is simply $S_o[(S_o - N)/S_o]^w$ where the total number of weak and strengthened synapses is S_o. We define the number of strengthened synapses in a neuron trained to recognize w patterns as N', and its mean is:

$$E[N'] = S_o - \left\{ S_o \left[(S_o - N)/S_o \right]^w \right\} = S_o \left[1 - \left(\frac{R-1}{R} \right)^w \right] \qquad (2.2)$$

Since Equation 2.2 ignores the fact that not all trained patterns may be learned, it tends to overestimate the number of strengthened synapses. A more accurate expression for p_F incorporates the binomial probability distribution P[k] for coin-toss experiments, where k "heads" result after n coins are tossed, each with the independent probability p of being heads:

$$P[k \mid n, p] = \binom{n}{k} p^k (1-p)^{n-k} \tag{2.3}$$

The notation:

$$\binom{n}{k} = \frac{n!}{k!(n-k)!} \tag{2.4}$$

which is commonly called "n choose k," signifies the number of unique ways one can choose k items from a list of n.

We separately define $P[N' \mid S_0, R, G, H, w]$ as the probability that a neuron has N' strengthened synapses after training on w patterns. It can be found by means of the following recursive equation in w, where w is initially zero.

$$P[N' \mid S_0, R, G, H, w] = \sum_{i=0}^{N'} P[i \mid S_0, R, G, H, w-1] \cdot$$

$$\sum_{j=0}^{i} [\theta(j \cdot G + (N'-j) - H) \cdot P(j \mid i, R^{-1}) \cdot P(N'-j \mid S_0 - i, R^{-1})]$$

$$+ \; P[N' \mid S_0, R, G, H, w] \cdot$$

$$\sum_{i=0}^{N'} \sum_{j=0}^{S_0 - N'} \left[(1 - \theta(i \cdot G + j - H)) \cdot P(i \mid N', R^{-1}) \cdot P(j \mid S_0 - N', R^{-1}) \right]$$

(2.5)

We define $P[N' \mid S_0, R, G, H, 0]$ to be unity when N' is zero, and zero otherwise; this reflects the fact that all neurons start (w = 0) with no strengthened synapses. The first summation on index i is over the probability that the neuron has i strengthened synapses after w – 1 patterns are trained. This sum is then multiplied by the sum over j of the probability of an input pattern having both j active synapses among the i strengthened synapses and N'- j active synapses among the S_o - i un-strengthened synapses; the function θ ensures that the sum includes only patterns that would cause the neuron to fire. $\theta(x)$ is a threshold function that equals zero for $x < 0$ and equals one for $x \geq 0$; and the factor $\theta(j \cdot G + (N'-j) - H)$ enforces the threshold condition that the weighted input summation must be equal to or greater than H. The second term accounts for cases where N' did not increase because the neuron did not fire.

We then calculate the expectation as the weighted sum:

$$E[N'] = \sum_{N'=0}^{S_0} N' \cdot P[N' | S_0, R, G, H, w] \tag{2.6}$$

Figure 2.3 plots $E[N']$ as a function of w for four values of $S_o/E[N'] = R$, where the number of synapses is $S_o = 1000$ and R here equals 10, 20, 30, or 40 and is also a variable used later. The figure makes clear that the desired fraction N'/S_o of strengthened synapses strongly limits w, the number of patterns taught and therefore learned. N'/S_o is limited in turn by the maximum desired rate p_F of false positive responses (an output spike) to a pattern that was not taught. Figure 2.3 also plots the experimentally obtained values of $E[N']$ as a function of w using the simulator, which is described later in Section 2.9 and Appendix B. In this case, the theoretical and experimental values for $E[N']$ are nearly indistinguishable.

The expression for p_F incorporates $P_{fire}(N' | S_0, R, G, H)$, the probability that a neuron with N' strengthened synapses will fire during recognition of a random input pattern:

$$P_{fire}(N' | S_0, R, G, H) = \sum_{i=0}^{N'} \left(P(i | S_0, R^{-1}) \cdot \sum_{j}^{S_0 - N'} \theta(i \cdot G + j - G \cdot H) \cdot P(j | S_0 - N', R^{-1}) \right) \tag{2.7}$$

We can now define $p_F[N' | w]$ as the probability that a neuron that was trained on w words and has N' strengthened neurons will fire in response to an unlearned input as:

24

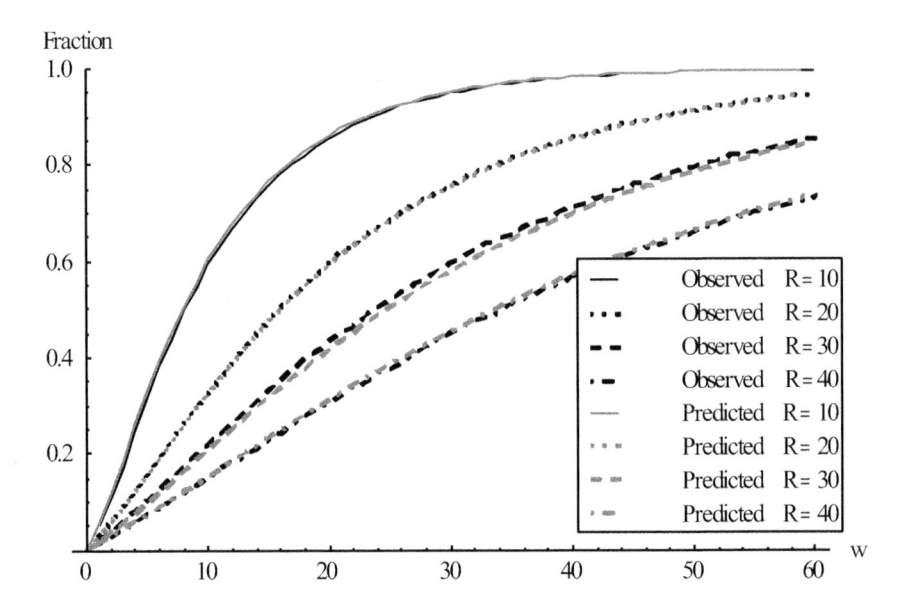

Figure 2.3 Expected value of N', the number of strengthened synapses, as a function of the number w of patterns trained.

$$p_F(N',w) = P_{fire}(N'|S_0,R,G,H) - \frac{w}{2^{N'}} \qquad (2.8)$$

We can now compute p_F as:

$$p_F(w|S_0,R,G,H) = \sum_{N'=0}^{S_0} \left(P[N'|S_0,R,G,H,w] \cdot p_F(N'|S_0,R,G,H,w) \right) \qquad (2.9)$$

Figure 2.4 shows the false positive probability p_F as a function of N' when S_o is 1000, G is 1.9, and $R = \overline{E[N']}/S_o$ is either 10, 20, 30, or 40. The false positive probability increases slowly and linearly at first as N' increases, and then faster when there are more strengthened synapses that the unlearned pattern might accidentally excite. p_F increases with R because N is then smaller with a relatively larger statistical tail.

Figure 2.5 shows the false positive probability p_F as a function of the number w of patterns taught when S_0 is 1000, G is 1.9, and R is one of 10,

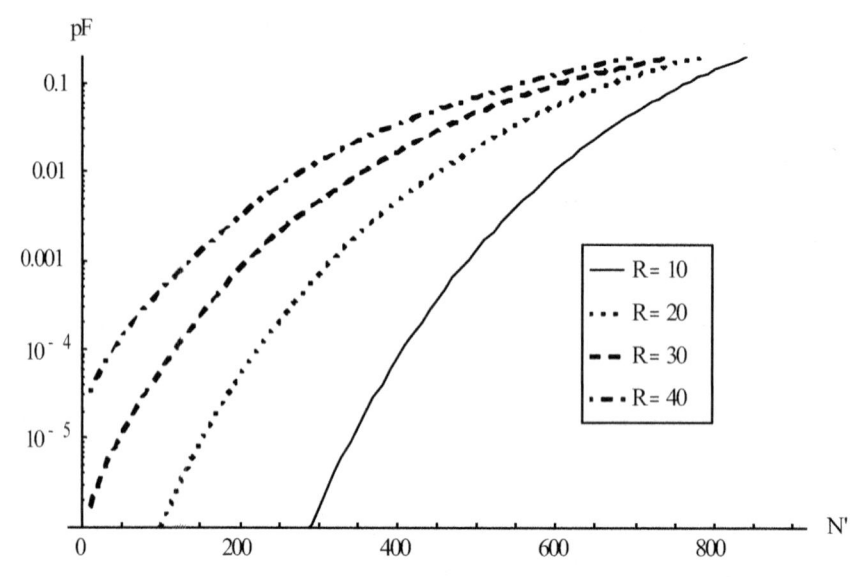

Figure 2.4 Probability p_F of a false positive response as a function of $N' = S_G$ when $S_o = 1000$, $G = 1.9$, and $R = \overline{N}/S_o$.

20, 30, or 40; only a fraction of those taught are learned. The figure shows that greater sparsity (larger values of $R = S_o/E[N']$) generally yields lower false positive rates p_F for p_F above ~0.1 percent. Theory and experiment are in generally good agreement.

This result demonstrates that a single basic neuron model can fairly reliably recognize multiple random patterns for $G < 2$. Bloom filters (Bloom, 1970) were developed within computer science and similarly extract multiple messages from sparse vectors. Bloom filters differ, however, in that they assume N is fixed whereas it is binomially distributed in cognons.

It is obviously more efficient if only one or a few neighboring neurons learn any given excitation pattern, rather than having excess duplication among many. Therefore it would be useful for a neuron that recognizes one pattern to suppress its nearby neighbors' ability to learn the same pattern. One common hypothesis is that this is partly accomplished if some fraction of all axons inhibit firing of nearby neurons by using synapses having negative strength.

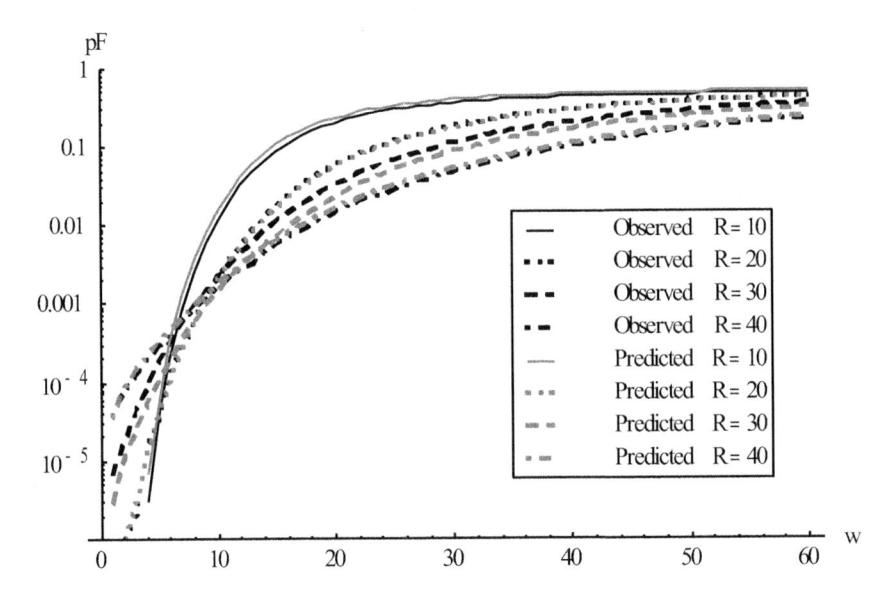

Figure 2.5: Probability of false positives as a function of w when $S_o = 1000$ and $G = 1.9$. Predicted curves are gray.

But what fraction of all synapses needs to be inhibitory? Let's arbitrarily assume that reducing the summed excitation by 20 percent suffices to prevent or terminate a given neuron's response to a pattern. This would suggest that roughly 10 percent of the input synapses have strength of -1, for example, instead of +1 or G.

This model assumes that the inhibition is applied to neurons at the same level as the originating neuron, so it can be tested by observing the degree to which inhibition is applied preferentially to real neurons in the same logical level or to those above or below. If inhibition is applied primarily to higher or lower levels it would be more difficult to learn how to inhibit excessively redundant pattern learning because the out-of-layer neurons respond to different types of features. If 10 percent of H synapses corresponds to one standard deviation of H when summed, this would imply that $H \cong 100$. Thus the percentage of inhibitory synapses, their computational purpose, and neural properties and connectivity are linked.

2.5 Recognition by layered spike-processing neural models

It is now natural to ask whether such recognition capabilities of single neurons are arguably sufficient for combinations of neurons to recognize still more complex patterns. Such hierarchical recognition strategies are widely assumed (e.g., Freiwald & Tsao, 2010; Hawkins & Blakeslee, 2004).

Imagine a multi-layer neural network where the first layer of neurons might have as its inputs black or white pixels in an extended visual field. Leaving aside for now the question of learning, the first layer might recognize only simple features within small local sectors of the visual field where, for example, first-layer neurons at the left end of the field might identify only those features confined to the left end. Some first-layer neurons might also respond to full-field parameters such as luminance. Neurons in the second layer might accept inputs from first-layer neurons that span more of the visual field and recognize more complex features (i.e., features of features) and those in the third layer might accept inputs from second-layer neurons anywhere. Obviously the complexity of features recognizable by third-layer neurons could be much greater than those recognizable by first-layer neurons.

Fortunately not all possible visual patterns are of interest. For example, the first layer of neurons might recognize several basic strokes that comprise typical letters of the alphabet (e.g., short straight and slightly curved lines at various angles, blank regions, and dots) while single neurons in the second layer might combine these strokes into letters of the alphabet at different positions and third-layer neurons might each recognize a different set of learned patterns.

Although the human visual system and other sensory systems are more complex, the basic principle of hierarchical recognition should be clear along with the notion that relatively few patterns (e.g., letters, patterns, or faces of friends) are likely to be useful at the highest layers so that neurons at the higher levels may have roughly the same complexity as those at the lower levels. Because the numbers of neurons in each level of the visual system are very roughly constant it follows that the numbers of recognizable patterns at each level may also be very roughly constant.

That is, the number of high-level concepts like "grandmother" might approximate the number of features recognizable at any lower level.

One of the main mathematical advantages of this basic neural recognition model has thus been demonstrated. Despite its simplicity (a binary threshold-firing neuron), it instantly spikes when it sees one of several trained patterns and only rarely otherwise. Its ability to recognize multiple patterns with low false-alarm probabilities is improved as the number of synapses, S_o, increases relative to the number N of spikes characterizing the trained patterns being recognized.

It is obviously more efficient if only one or a few neighboring neurons learn any given excitation pattern, rather than having excess duplication among many. Therefore it would be useful for a neuron that recognizes one pattern to suppress its nearby neighbors' ability to learn the same pattern. One common hypothesis is that this is partly accomplished if some fraction of axons inhibit firing of nearby neurons by using synapses that have negative strength.

But what fraction of all synapses needs to be inhibitory? Let's arbitrarily assume that reducing the summed excitation by 20 percent suffices to prevent or terminate a given neuron's response to a pattern. This would suggest that roughly 10 percent of the input synapses have strength of -1 or -G, for example, instead of +1 or G.

This model assumes that the inhibition is applied to neurons at the same level as the originating neuron, so it can be tested by observing the degree to which inhibition is applied preferentially to real neurons in the same logical level or to those above or below. If inhibition is applied primarily to higher or lower levels it would be more difficult to learn how to inhibit excessively redundant pattern learning because the out-of-layer neurons respond to different types of features. If 10 percent of H synapses corresponds to one standard deviation of H when summed, this would imply that $H \cong 100$. Thus the percentage of inhibitory synapses, their computational purpose, and neural properties and connectivity are linked.

2.6 Basic spike-processing neural learning model

So far we have seen that the identities of learned patterns can be imbedded in the input (afferent) synapse strengths, e.g. unity versus the gain G, but we have not discussed how this basic neural recognition model could learn new patterns or determines which ones to learn.

The main constraint we impose for any computational learning model is that it must support sub-second learning in a manner arguably consistent with neural observations. Our basic learning model utilizes a simplified form of spike-timing-dependent plasticity (STDP) for which any spike that arrives in a timely way so as to help trigger an output spike instantly strengthens its synapse from a weight of unity to G ($G > 1$), as discussed earlier. Since the basic model is binary, no other synapse strengths are allowed. We designate this as the synapse-strength (SS) learning model.

The assumed SS learning mechanism is that when a learning-ready neuron is being trained, any pattern that excites an output spike also irreversibly strengthens the weights of all contributing afferent synapses from 1 to G. The neurological basis for this assumption is that spike-triggered dendritic back-propagation is known to strengthen afferent synapses (Markram, Lubke, Frotscher, & Sakmann, 1997; Bi & Poo, 1998). Although it is unknown how markedly synapse strengths can change *in vivo* based on a single spike, G values less than two seem arguably plausible and consistent with limited observations; the simulation results presented later in Tables 2.3 and 2.4 show that these values yield acceptable learning and retrieval performance.

This "instant learning" model avoids the mathematical NP-complete back-propagation training time barrier (neuron learning times increase roughly exponentially with the number of synapses per neuron) because learning is accomplished almost instantly within a single neuron rather than requiring tedious interactions between pairs of neurons. This roughly assumes that any pattern presented to a neuron while it is learning ready or plastic merits memorization.

This SS basic learning model raises two key questions: 1) what neurological mechanisms might permit a transition between the neuron's normal state where it is merely seeking to recognize input patterns, and its learning-ready state where it seeks to memorize all patterns, or the fraction p_L, that trigger an output spike, and 2) what cognitive means might select those time intervals and cortical regions that should undertake memorization to promote animal well being?

Although neuron firing thresholds in nature vary with time, they are difficult to observe experimentally. In the absence of contrary data the basic SS learning model therefore simply assumes that the neural firing thresholds in those cortical regions being trained are temporarily lowered slightly from their recognition level of $G \cdot H$ to H during learning readiness, thus increasing p_L, the probability of learning. With lower firing thresholds it becomes much easier for novel patterns to fire the neuron and thereby be learned.

But what regions of the cortex are being trained? One clue may be the instantaneously active but spatially constrained regions revealed by functional MRI images (fMRI). fMRI responds primarily to local metabolic activity that indicates currently active areas where firing thresholds could plausibly be temporarily altered. Another possibility is that astrocytes might additionally modulate the firing threshold for those neurons to which they are connected. Astrocytes are glial cells intimately mixed with neurons and that receive inputs from both the blood stream and local axons and that link to dendritic spines near synapses; they are also known to modulate plasticity and learning (Volterra & Meldolesi, 2005; Panatier et al., 2006).

We saw earlier that if G were sufficiently large, neurons could recognize many trained patterns while still exhibiting small probabilities of false alarm due to untaught signals. Therefore we assume here for computational simplicity that for any value of G the firing threshold is either its learning-ready value of H or its non-learning recall value of $G \cdot H$. This assumption preserves the ratio between the firing threshold and the weighted sum for any recognizable pattern since both are multiplied by G. Other synapses with unity weight are therefore disadvantaged by a factor of G where, constrained by homology, the simulated optimum values for G presented later in Section 2.8 often lie in the range $1.3 < G < 1.8$, which is arguably consistent with *in vivo* observations; without homology, higher G

values generally perform better although values below 2 generally perform nearly as well (see Table 2.3).

This basic learning neuron model makes the simplifying assumption that synapses do not increase in strength when the neuron is not learning ready; omitting this assumption would lead to optimum values for G somewhat greater than those presented later in Tables 2.3 and 2.4 in Section 2.8, and these values would increase monotically with time as all synapse strengths eventually become equal to G. Since having the same G for all synapses is clearly suboptimal it seems more reasonable to assume that learning readiness of neurons is somehow controlled so that w does not exceed its optimum limits.

This basic learning SS neuron model is supplemented by another neurologically plausible instant learning model in Section 3.1 that may operate in combination with an SS mechanism. The first instant learning neural model, however, was the Willshaw model (Willshaw, Buneman, & Longuet-Higgins, 1969; Graham & Willshaw, 1999), which assumed that learning was accomplished by applying simultaneously to both the inputs and the outputs of a layer of neurons a pair of patterns that were to be associated. Afferent synapses that fired concurrently with their output neuron during training were then irreversibly strengthened from zero to unity. The difficulty with the Willshaw model is that there is as yet no arguably plausible useful source for the necessary output excitation patterns.

In contrast, our basic learning neuron model explicitly uses only the neuron input excitation patterns for providing this information, where the probability for learning a pattern during learning readiness is generally less than one. Learning is enabled by a separate learning readiness signal that either lowers the firing threshold or, equivalently, raises the general excitation and number of spikes produced in that neural neighborhood, thus positively biasing sums computed there, albeit with additional shot noise (shot noise arises when one sums E random events; the sum's root-mean-square [rms] variation commonly approximates $E^{0.5}$).

The efficiency of learning can be further increased by the same or a separate signal that enables synaptic plasticity only when that cortical region is sensing patterns with survival implications or even paying attention. An example of a survival-relevant hormone is adrenaline, and a likely cellular means for altering plasticity in neurons is astrocytes, as discussed above.

Although all "instant-learning" models can learn excitation patterns upon one exposure, slower learning models could utilize repetitive exposures, each of which triggers a smaller change in synaptic strength (Milner, Squire, & Kandel, 1998; Markram et al., 1997).

At this point we can define the cognon family of neuron models and its major variants and abbreviations. A cognon is a neuron model that for each nearly instantaneous excitation pattern at its afferent synapses: 1) weights each incoming constant amplitude spikes by its corresponding synapse strength and if the summed result exceeds a firing threshold that may vary with time, then the neuron fires its own spike; no more than one spike arrives at each synapse per excitation pattern, 2) increases the strength of those synapses that had not yet reached maximum strength and that contributed to the generation of an output spike while the neuron was learning ready, and 3) reveals no more information per output spike beyond the fact that the responsible input excitation pattern was probably among those exposed to the neuron earlier when it was learning ready.

Two major categories of cognons are the cognon-basic (CB) models described above, and the cognon-extended (CE) models that add to the CB models such possibilities as $C > 1$, $D > 1$, and additional but similar learning models.

The next step is to validate the basic cognon learning model using simulations, but it is useful to have one or more performance metrics, one of which can be the Shannon information (bits) that can be learned and then recalled by a single basic neuron model employing "synaptic strength learning" (SS).

2.7. Shannon information metric

Given that simple neurons can respond with spikes to learned patterns while not responding to most others, what is the Shannon information

(Shannon, 1948) that can be extracted from those neurons? Such information is commonly measured in bits, where one bit equals the information conveyed by one flip of a random coin; this is a widely used measure for information storage and communication rates. Shannon defined the average information I in a representative message or pattern as:

$$I = -\sum_{i} p_i \log_2 p_i \quad \text{(bits)} \tag{2.10}$$

where p_i is the probability that pattern i constitutes the message. In the ideal limit where $N = H$ and only one pattern is learned, only that learned pattern can always be recognized perfectly, and there can never be any false alarms despite there being $2^{S_o} - 1$ possible false patterns. To communicate the maximum information, all such perfectly recognizable patterns should be equally likely to be sent or learned. In this case a single such correctly recognized learned pattern conveys S_o bits:

$$I = -\sum_{i=1}^{2^{S_o}} 2^{-S_o} \log_2 2^{-S_o} = \sum_{i=1}^{2^{S_o}} S_o 2^{-S_o} = S_o \quad \text{(bits)} \tag{2.11}$$

Thus the number of bits recallable from a binary neuron cannot exceed the number of its binary synapses, S_o; this is also intuitively obvious without reference to the equations. Nor is there any other useful way to extract information from such a simple static neuron—it either spikes in response to an input pattern or it doesn't; it has no ability to distinguish time sequences. If the messages are not equally likely, then the sum in (2.11) is diminished because the full message space is not being used efficiently.

This upper bound on I for a perfectly trained binary neuron assumed perfect recognition. In fact, false alarms reduce $I = L$, as derived in Section 3.2. Moreover, neurons may not learn perfectly every pattern they see during training. Before discussing learning models in more detail let's quickly define recallable learned information L (bits) for a simple binary neural model that learns new excitation patterns with learning probability $p_L \leq 1$.

The recallable learned information is the mutual information $L = I(\bar{X}, \bar{Y})$ (bits) between the set $\bar{X}$ of possible excitation patterns that was taught to single neurons, but not necessarily learned, and the set $\bar{Y}$ of patterns that each neuron recognizes, but was not necessarily taught. The same mutual information metric was applied to neurons by Barrett and van Rossum (2008). Since the details of this equation are not critical to a general understanding of the model and its performance, they may be skipped for now if they are obscure. The main point is that the maximum taught information L (bits) recallable from such simple neural models is reduced by failures to learn what was taught (i.e., the probability of learning $p_L < 1$) and by responses to patterns that were not taught (i.e., the false alarm probability $p_F > 0$). Equation 2.12 is derived briefly in Section 3.2 and more thoroughly in Appendix B, and is:

$$L \cong w \left[(1 - p_L) \log_2 \frac{1 - p_L}{1 - p_F} + p_L \log_2 \frac{p_L}{p_F} \right] \text{ bits} \qquad (2.12)$$

where w is the number of patterns taught but not necessarily learned.

The most interesting result revealed by Equation 2.12 is that the recoverable information L is zero if $p_F \geq p_L$ since L cannot be negative. This makes sense. If the neuron responds only to the fraction p_L of taught patterns during training, and the response rate during recall is the same for random patterns as for those learned, then there is no way to distinguish learned information from noise since they respond with the same statistics. The CB neural model ensures that $p_F < p_L$ by increasing both the original strength of the trained synapses and the firing threshold during recall by the factor G, which reduces p_F. The Willshaw model and the synapse atrophy (SA) CE learning model introduced later effectively do the same with $G \to \infty$.

The total information recoverable from any neural network containing M neurons is always bounded from above by ML, where L is the average information recallable from each neuron. This is analogous to computer memories for which the total recoverable information in bits cannot exceed the sum of the information in each subunit of that memory.

2.8 Simulations of the cognon basic (CB) learning model

The simulations of the CB learning model presented here arbitrarily assume that: 1) the number of afferent synapses is fixed at S_o, 2) the probability that any given synapse is excited for any particular excitation pattern is $1/R$ and is independent and identically distributed among synapses and patterns, 3) the learning-readiness firing threshold is H and the threshold during recall is $G \cdot H$, and 4) the number of taught patterns is w, where not all taught patterns are learned. The results are expressed in terms of the probabilities of learning p_L, the false alarm probability p_F, and the maximum stored information L, as given by Equation (2.4).

The values for p_F presented in Table 2.1 were based on the given parameters N, H, S_o, w, and G, which were not numerically optimized. Optimization is now possible because the metrics L (bits/neuron) and L/S_o (bits/synapse) introduced in Section 2.7 are directly relevant to neuron pattern recognition performance. For illustrative purposes we fixed the values of S_o and H while the variables R, w, and G were chosen to maximize L and L/S_o for each such combination of inputs. The results are shown in Table 2.3, where the probability of false alarm is the sum of p_F and its rms accuracy as estimated from the scatter among many results.

These optimizations were for representative values of H, S_o, and R that arguably overlap those of real neurons, at least partially. The optimized parameters w and G were restricted to discrete values in any combination, i.e.: $w = \{10, 20, 30,...,90, 100, 200, 300,..., 900, 1000, 2000, 3000, ..., 10,000\}$ and $G = \{1.0, 1.1, 1.2,....1.9, 2.0, 2.2, 2.4,...,4.0\}$.

The main result of Table 2.3 is that the CB neuron model can recall 157 bits of information if there are 1000 synapses ($p_F = 1.25\%$) and 33 bits if there are 200, which corresponds to approximately 0.16 bits per synapse when $G = 3.6$. Even with the synapse strength ratio G as low as 1.9 this model can recall 104 bits from 1000 synapses ($p_F = 2.4\%$) and 9 bits from 200 synapses, which corresponds to 0.1 and 0.045 bits per synapse, respectively. These values for bits/synapse are on the same order as

Table 2.3. Values of L, p_F, and p_L as a function of the CB model parameters.

L	$p_F(\%)$	$p_L(\%)$	H	G	S_o	R	w
710	1.42	72.3	30	4.0	10,000	303	200
448	0.10	85.3	105	4.0	10,000	86	70
315	0.18	0.52	40	1.9	10,000	250	100
157	1.25	18.9	5	3.6	1000	333	300
112	1.06	0.42	10	3.6	1000	111	60
104	2.42	18.8	5	1.9	1000	333	300
94.3	0.52*	55.4	15	4.0	1000	66	30
33.0	2.10*	28.0	5	3.6	200	57	40
23.1	3.02*	56.3	10	4.0	200	20	10
9.52	1.57*	25.0	20	1.9	200	12	10

* p_F rms > 0.5 p_F

estimates made for other neural and information models (Baldassi, Braunstein, Brunel, & Zecchina, 2007; Barrett & van Rossum, 2008).

The values in Table 2.3 are lower than those in Table 2.1 because: 1) $G = 1.9$ and $G = 4$ are both more consistent with neural observations and well below the value of 100 assumed in Table 2.1, and 2) the number N of excited synapses was specified in Table 2.1 but is now binomially distributed about its mean S_o/R. As a result there are learning losses, particularly when $N < H$ so that $p_L = 0$, and extra false alarm losses when the tail of the N distribution exceeds H by larger margins. In Table 2.1 there were no learning losses since $p_L = 1$ because the learned patterns were imbedded in the synaptic weights from the beginning.

The value of having 10,000 synapses is more apparent for the extended cognon models discussed in Chapter 3.

Table 2.3 also suggests that lower values of H permit storage of more information per neuron and synapse, which makes sense since more unique patterns can be learned before the number of strengthened synapses becomes so large that false alarms preclude more learning. The table also suggests that the product $H \cdot R \cong S_o$, which also makes sense because an average of S_o/R synapses fire per pattern and this should approximate the firing threshold H.

The values of H and R presented in the table are arguably consistent with nature. For example, in real neurons the firing threshold H might reasonably range between ~60, a nominal ratio of threshold-to-single-spike voltages, and ~9, a nominal ratio of threshold-to-single-spike currents, the currents being more relevant to slower signals (Koch, 1999). The number of synapses S_o varies among species and neuron types and can exceed 100,000 in humans. If the period T between excitation patterns approximates that for gamma waves, say 30 msec, then observed ~150-3000 msec intervals (say) between consecutive spikes for attentive animals would imply that the average rate R lies roughly between 5 and 100 input patterns presented per output spike produced. Most values in the table are consistent with these estimates.

There is a potential constraint we have ignored, however. This follows from the observation that average neuron-spiking frequencies are roughly similar across the active cortex even though spike-based signals propagate across many logical layers when traversing multiple regions, like V1, V2, etc., in the visual cortex. For spike frequencies to be approximately layer-independent requires that the average value of R be approximately the same at both the input and output of any neural layer, a constraint we arbitrarily call "homology."

Homology requires that both the input and the output firing rates per pattern presented approximate $1/R$ (R = patterns presented per spike elicited). But during learning the output spiking rate is $1/R \cong p_L$ (probability that a presented pattern will be learned). This simple additional constraint leads to stable maximum values of the expected values of L and the associated optimum values for p_F, p_L, G, w, S_o, and S_G as functions of H and R, as tabulated in Table 2.4. $S_G = E[N']$ corresponds to the average number of synapses that have strength G after w patterns have been taught (but not necessarily learned, since $p_L < 1$).

Interesting conclusions drawn from this table include:

1) The optimum ratio between the minimum and maximum binary synapse strengths varies between 1.3 and 1.8 for these examples, which is arguably within the range observed in nature.

2) Up to ten bits can be learned and recalled by the CB neuron model when it is constrained by homology (say $0.6 < R \cdot p_L < 1.2$). The corresponding bits per synapse range up to 0.048. The homology

Table 2.4. Maximized values of L (bits/neuron) as a function of the CB model parameters and constrained by homology ($p_L \cdot R \cong 1$)

H	R	L	S_o	S_G	G	p_F (%)	$p_L \cdot R$	w
10	10	4.8	70	12	1.8	1.6*	1.14	10
10	20	7.8	120	19	1.7	0.84*	0.84	40
10	30	6.7	150	23	1.8	0.19*	0.53	100
10	40	6.4	200	20	1.6	0.08*	0.78	90
20	10	6.4	160	28	1.8	1.04*	1.16	10
20	20	8.9	280	50	1.7	0.85*	0.73	50
20	30	5.8	360	49	1.5	0.06*	0.49	100
20	40	4.7	480	40	1.5	0.01*	0.59	100
30	10	5.5	240	59	1.8	2.4*	0.72	20
30	20	6.4	420	66	1.3	0.45*	0.31	100
30	30	9.9	630	91	1.4	0.22*	1.28	100
30	40	8.8	840	99	1.7	0.03*	0.73	100
40	10	4.8	320	66	1.4	0.71*	0.62	20
40	20	10.5	640	207	1.4	0.73*	1.85	40
40	30	4.87	840	197	1.7	0.09*	0.71	100
40	40	3.41	1120	93	1.5	0.00*	0.71	100

* p_F rms $> 0.5\, p_F$

constraint appears to be the limiting factor relative to the superior results of Table 2.3 since all parameters other than H and R are roughly optimized in Table 2.4.

3) Under homology the maximum number L of recallable bits per neuron is surprisingly independent of its firing threshold H and the firing rate per random input pattern, $1/R$, whereas the bits per synapse vary two orders of magnitude.

4) The optimum false alarm probability p_F under these assumptions is roughly 1 percent while the corresponding learning probability p_L lies between 1.5 and 11 percent.

5) The number w of patterns taught varies between 10 and 100, which corresponds to $p_L w$ patterns learned, or roughly between one and three patterns per homologous neuron.

6) The optimum fraction S_G/S_o of strong synapses when fully trained lies between 8 and 32 percent.

7) To learn 10 bits might require a minimum of $\tau = R/\gamma p_L$ seconds, where γ is the pattern presentation frequency; if $\gamma = 30$ Hz, then $\tau \geq \sim 7$ seconds for a homologous neuron model with 840 synapses.

8) Less apparent from Table 2.4 is that most patterns are learned in the extended (fat) tails of output spiking-probability distributions where averages of p_F across multiple trials are more volatile than they would be for Gaussian distributions. This is why the rms values for p_F are often large compared to p_F, as indicated by "*".

Comparison of Tables 2.3 and 2.4 makes clear that the assumed form of homology substantially reduces the information capacity of these CB neurons. This result raises the question of the time scales on which homology might be obeyed, because the results in Table 2.3 without homology were roughly an order of magnitude better.

Homology was imposed on the CB model to ensure that the average spiking rate for Table 2.4 was approximately the same at all levels of a neural network, consistent with cortical observations. But if the spiking rate were high (low values of R) only during learning, and were lower during recognition (higher values of R), neural performance could be significantly improved. Since only one layer is presumably trained at a time in a given local area, temporarily high values of R during learning could be consistent with long-term homology.

For example, by dropping the threshold H sufficiently during learning, nearly every pattern could be learned so $p_L > 0.5$. Then by raising H during recognition, R could become quite high and thus violate the homology constraint $p_L \cdot R \cong 1$. But such bursts in R would be averaged over long time periods and go unnoticed when computing long-term $p_L \cdot R$. For example, if $p_F = 0.01$, $p_L = 1$, and $p_F \cdot R = 0.3$ (corresponding to useful p_F), then the homology metric $p_L \cdot R = 30$ rather than 1, which significantly increases L and most other useful neural metrics above the values of Table 2.4 (see Table 2.3).

2.9 Summary and next steps

Chapter 2 has shown how a simple binary threshold-firing neural model using binary synapse-strength (SS) learning can learn multiple binary patterns by one-time exposures to each such pattern sufficient to generate an output spike. When synapses learn new patterns they are strengthened irreversibly from unity to $G > 1$ as a result of one (or more) of its spikes contributing to the sum responsible for the output spike produced when that pattern is learned.

Only a fraction p_L of such "taught" patterns are learned, however, because not all patterns can generate an output spike. This is because spikes are generated independently and randomly by the input neurons, and therefore the number N of incident spikes that defines a pattern is a random variable and is sometimes below H, which precludes learning unless some pattern-excited synapses have already been strengthened. If the firing threshold increases to more than $H \cdot G$ during recall, the number of these few learned but unrecallable patterns can perhaps be diminished. Small learning probabilities p_L could be readily compensated if the density of neurons within each layer is sufficiently high that at least a few neurons within a given area typically responded to any pattern of interest. Once learned, such patterns should always elicit an output spike from at least a few neighboring neurons when these patterns are presented during recall.

The distinction between learning and recall for SS learning is that the firing threshold is H during learning and $G \cdot H$, $G > 1$ during recall, which is necessary in order to reduce the false-alarm probability p_F significantly below the probability of learning p_L; otherwise, information theory suggests in Equation 2.7 that useful information cannot be recovered.

To summarize further, this section demonstrated the significant mathematical advantages of this CB neural model. It not only instantly responds with a spike to any of a set of trained patterns, but also can instantly train additional novel patterns by temporarily lowering its firing threshold from its recognition value of $G \cdot H$ to its learning-ready value H during the training session. Equivalently all spike amplitudes could alternatively be increased via neurotransmitters by the same factor G. At the same time the false-alarm probability p_F that an untrained pattern might erroneously trigger a recognition spike can be made sufficiently small by increasing G so that the learning metric L is not unduly degraded in Equation 2.12. Moreover, the required value of G is arguably within the range observed in nature, i.e., less than a factor of two. Further reductions in p_F are available by decreasing the number w of patterns trained.

At this point skeptics might raise three issues that have ready responses. First, this result is not just a theory since the model's power to rapidly learn and later recall new patterns with high reliability and low false alarm probabilities has been demonstrated here by simulations readily duplicated by others (see Tables 2.1, 2.3, and 2.4 and Appendix B).

Second, although some might question the choice of information metric L, it follows directly from information theory and our minimalist assumption that the only information conveyed by an output spike is that the neuron saw a similar pattern during training or learning readiness. Other information metrics would apply if the time intervals between successive output spikes conveyed information, or if the probability of an output spike was a function of the time sequence of recent output spikes or excitation patterns.

Also, the utility of the cognon model lies in the speed and reliability of its learning and recall of complex patterns, independent of the definition of L. Moreover, although single neurons have limited recognition capabilities, multiple neurons arranged in layers can collectively learn to recognize patterns of almost arbitrary complexity. Such randomly wired neuron layers can be trained in succession shortly after birth when the environment is first viewed, as discussed in Section 2.6; training of any layer would generally begin at birth when the environment is first viewed, but not until its input layer were trained and no longer fully plastic.

Third, some current theories regarding cortex require neural outputs to characterize their excitation patterns in some way beyond a simple "spike or no spike." The CB model simulations presented here and their high values for the associated Shannon information metric suggest this is not necessary, which is fortunate since there are no current plausible theories about how such a complex characterization of neural inputs might occur other than via the feedback model discussed later in Chapter 5, which employs this same CB model.

Chapter 3 revisits these issues more thoroughly and with a more elaborate neural model that allows for multiple fixed spike times within patterns and for dendritic compartments that can fire independently. It also introduces new learning models and elaborates on possible similarities between these neural models and traditional neuroscience.

Chapter 3
Full neural model

3.1. Extensions of the cognon neural model

It is useful to see if extensions of the mathematical complexity of the CB model might have utility, particularly if experiments have suggested such extensions might have approximate counterparts in nature.

The first such extension follows from the observation that in nature some synapses can sum their excitations more effectively when those synapses are close together, while some may sum their excitations more effectively when far apart (London & Hausser, 2005; Rall, 1977). We can roughly approximate such behavior by assuming there are $C \geq 1$ "compartments" per neuron, and the synapse excitations are separately summed within each of them and tested against H during learning or against $G \cdot H$ during recognition. If one or more compartments fire then the model neuron also immediately fires, and back-propagation within each firing compartment strengthens its untrained plastic synapses that contributed to that firing; all other synapses remain unchanged, including those that were excited within compartments that did not fire.

The second extension is more complex for it assumes that fixed differences in propagation times between neurons can introduce small time offsets in spike arrival times. The consequence of this is that for each neural excitation pattern there may be more than one narrow time slot of roughly 1-3 msec duration within which the excitations are summed and tested against the threshold H (during training) or $G \cdot H$ (during recall). Many observations have strongly suggested that some neurons code spike-based patterns using such variable delays (Brown, Kass, & Mitra; 2004, Kozhevnikov & Fee, 2007; Coleman & Sarma, 2010).

If successive patterns are presented for recognition at a nominal period of 25 milliseconds, which characterizes the gamma band evidenced in EEG data, then a few such resolvable time slots would be available per pattern, permitting multiple summations and logic operations per pattern. We define D to be the effective number of resolvable time delays characterizing the spikes produced by a single neuron in response to a single pattern, and D' to be the effective number of resolvable time delays characterizing the set of propagation paths and delays between the point of summation and the outputs (soma) of those neurons exciting the neuron of interest. Thus, the total number of possible delays between the input neuron and the point of summation is $D + D' - 1$. Usually $D' > D$ if $D > 1$, for reasons discussed later. Note that if $C = D = D' = 1$, we simply have the CB model discussed in Chapter 2.

Figure 3.1 illustrates the extended CE model, analogous to Figure 2.1. The main additions are the explicit recognition that: 1) the cumulative time-invariant delay in the axon, synapse, and dendrite path conveying any particular spike can differ because of its unique link length, synapse location on the dendrite, or biochemical dynamics, and 2) the dendrite arbor may be divided into compartments that, in this mathematical simplification, fire and train independently, as discussed below.

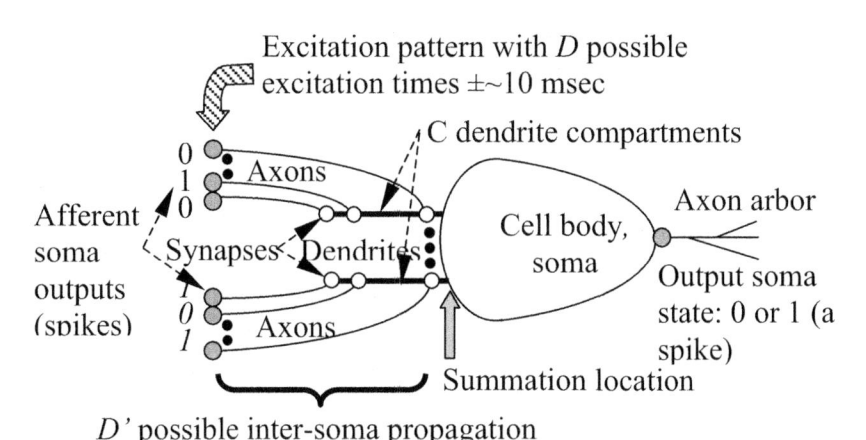

Figure 3.1. CE model showing D possible excitation delays and D' possible inter-soma propagation delays.

A physically plausible dendrite compartment might, for example, be an independent dendrite branch feeding the cell body directly. A neuron might have C such compartments, as discussed above.

Figure 3.2 shows how the pattern definition and timing in Figure 2.2 might be altered if $D = 2$. It explicitly shows how a single pattern might include some exciting spikes that are generated a little late so that they must be brought into coincidence by correspondingly shorter propagation times in their axon/synapse/dendrite link in order to sum efficiently to surpass the firing threshold. Pattern A exhibits two spikes that leave their incident neurons a few milliseconds late; the horizontal axis of the figure represents time. But pattern C shows that the delays in those two paths are correspondingly shorter so the generation and propagation delays cancel and coincidence results. If they did not cancel, these spikes could not have contributed coherently to the sum that triggered firing during learning readiness; those synapses would therefore not have been strengthened at that time.

When the number D of possible small delay increments within a pattern exceeds unity, it implies that spikes arriving from separate input neurons must be well synchronized or they could be misinterpreted. One possible mechanism is synchronization to an event earlier in the neural chain, such as might be initiated by a saccade (Gollisch & Meister, 2008) as the eye flicks back and forth, or by timing mechanisms in the thalamus or elsewhere.

Since information is embedded in the combination of relative delays between each of a pattern's input spikes, and in the exact population of input neurons that constitute a given pattern fed to a given neuron, this type of pattern coding is designated a population-delay code and has been proposed by others (Bohte, 2004; Hopfield, Brody, & Roweis, 1998). Other proposed signal coding means include pulse rate coding, population coding, and delay coding (Berger & Levy, 2010); but we explore the consequences of only population coding (Averbeck, Latham, & Pouget, 2006), which is used by the CB model, and of population delay coding, which is used by the CE model.

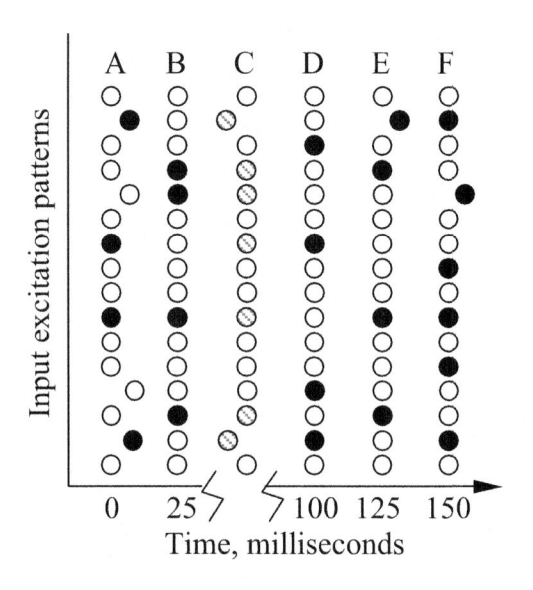

Figure 3.2. Pattern timing diagram for $D = 2$. Each pattern has 16 input neurons driving 16 synapses every 25 milliseconds. Spikes (black circles) can arrive at $D = 2$ possible times, as illustrated, and to synchronize their summation requires that each delayed input spike must be compensated by a reduced propagation delay within the inter-soma path, as illustrated by the hatched circles in the inter-neuron delays shown in pattern C that indicate the strong synapses ($G > 1$) that resulted when this neuron learned both patterns A and B earlier (black circles). Patterns D, E, and F are recognition test patterns (black circles) that produce excitation sums of G, $4G = G \cdot H$, and G, respectively, where only pattern E causes a false alarm because four of its black dots correspond to four hatched dots in C.

The third extension of the CB model involves addition of a new learning mechanism, designated the synapse atrophy (SA) learning model. It can function alone or in combination with the synapse strength (SS) CB model, where the combination appears to be likely. Such a combination can help reduce the average false-alarm rate of the synapse strength model, which arises partly from the fact that those synapses with reduced weight (unity) still contribute to the sum which is tested against the threshold $G \cdot H$ and can therefore cause the neuron to fire erroneously.

Little would probably be lost if those synapses that never contributed to a spike during learning, despite many opportunities, atrophied to make space for new synapses. Such continual replacement of less useful synapses with potentially more useful ones linked to other neurons could maintain the total number of synapses per neuron roughly constant over most of each neuron's life. The number of synapses on young neurons typically increases with time and then slowly declines as the neuron becomes old, perhaps after years or decades.

The SA learning model could also function alone without the SS learning model, and its performance then resembles that of the Willshaw model discussed in Section 2.4, which exhibits high-performance instant learning, particularly when there are many neurons of which only a small fraction is typically excited at once. In both the synapse atrophy and Willshaw model all synapses have unity strength throughout training, but that strength becomes immortal if that synapse contributes to an output spike during learning, much as such synapses increase their strength to G for the SS model under similar circumstances.

In this case the learning probability p_L and the false alarm probability p_F remain equal, causing the recallable learned information L to be zero unless p_F is reduced significantly. p_F is easily reduced if the mortal (unenhanced) synapses atrophy (strength becomes zero) prior to measuring recognition performance. The SA simulation results presented later show the considerable benefits of such atrophy, as presaged by the early Willshaw results. As mentioned earlier, the Willshaw model unfortunately did not propose a neurologically plausible learning process, unlike the CB model introduced here.

The next section derives the learned information metric L (bits) for a single neuron, which was introduced in Equation 2.3 and Section 2.7. The derivation in Section 3.2 reveals some of the subtleties that lie behind the definition of information useful for cortical computations, but they need not concern us now with respect to the main thrust of this monograph.

3.2 Issues in derivation of the information stored per neuron

We assumed earlier that the learned Shannon information L (bits/neuron) recoverable from a binary neuron could only be derived from observations of which excitation patterns excite the neuron to spike. The sequence of test patterns used to extract this information does not matter if such testing does not change any synapse strengths. In this case L is the mutual information $I(\overline{X},\overline{Y})$ between the set $\overline{X}$ of binary excitation patterns "taught" while the neuron was learning-ready and plastic, and the set $\overline{Y}$ of those "learned" excitation patterns that stimulate output responses in non-plastic neurons. This neural mutual information metric has been used previously (e.g., Barrett & van Rossum, 2008).

A metaphorical example from communications theory is the following. Assume that Alice (proxy for the environment) wishes to tell Bob (proxy for the neural network) something that Bob should know (memorize) about his environment, and that she does this by means of a single new neuron that she trains. She trains that neuron while it is plastic by exposing it to a set of w patterns she chooses from a set of size $z \gg w$. She can choose $q = z!/[w!(z-w)!]$ possible unique pattern sets, where $\log_2 q$ (bits) is then the upper bound on retrievable information (Shannon, 1948).

Bob then extracts that maximum information by exposing the neuron to all z possible patterns and noting which patterns produce recognition signatures and are therefore presumed to have been selected and taught by Alice. Although information extraction could be tedious if all z patterns were tested, it can be greatly accelerated, perhaps even to ~1 bit/second, if the set of tested patterns is somehow restricted to that very limited set likely to occur in practice, as discussed later.

We earlier defined the learning probability p_L as the probability that a taught pattern will be learned, and defined the false alarm probability p_F as the probability that during recall Bob will see an output spike signature for a pattern that was not taught, where both the learning and recall imperfections reduce L below the theoretical limit $\log_2 q$. We assume that Alice and Bob know only the "name" of each pattern but cannot access the pattern's more extensive binary description or otherwise determine which patterns are correlated. They have access only to one isolated neuron at a time. We further ignore any information related to the relative sequence of any two patterns presented during recall, since synapse strengths are then fixed for both the SS and SA learning models so that the testing sequence does not matter.

Restricting the evaluation of recoverable information to that in a single neuron is useful because the total neural network system information cannot exceed the sum of the information recoverable from each neuron separately; correlations between neurons can only reduce that sum.

L can readily be evaluated under these assumptions. Let x_i and y_i be binary (0,1), where $x_i = 1$ signifies that the ith pattern was taught by Alice, but not whether it was learned, and $y_i = 1$ signifies that the same pattern produces a spike signature for Bob. Then, since time sequencing does not matter here, and for other reasons discussed below, the mutual information L (bits) is z times the mutual information L_l for each pattern alone:

$$\begin{aligned} L &= I(\overline{X},\overline{Y}) \\ &= z \cdot L_i \\ &= z \cdot I(x_i, y_i) \\ &= z \sum_{i,j \in \{0,1\}} P\{x_i, y_j\} \log_2 \frac{P\{x_i, y_j\}}{P\{x_i\}P\{y_j\}} \end{aligned} \quad (3.1)$$

where:

$$P\{x_i = 1\} \equiv p_T \ll 1 \quad (3.2)$$

and where p_T is the probability that Alice would teach a particular pattern (i.e., present that pattern to the neuron, which may not learn it), and

$$P\{y_i = 1 \mid x_i = 0\} \equiv p_F \quad (3.3)$$

$$P\{y_i = 1 \mid x_i = 1\} \equiv p_L \quad (3.4)$$

$$P\{y_i = 1\} = p_F(1 - p_T) + p_L p_T \quad (3.5)$$

The main result (3.6) follows by substituting (3.2)-(3.5) and simply inserting the related equations into Equation (3.1) while assuming $p_T \ll p_F$ so that the Taylor expansion can be used, as detailed below:

$$L \cong w\left[(1-p_L)\log_2 \frac{1-p_L}{1-p_F} + p_L\log_2 \frac{p_L}{p_F}\right] \text{ bits} \qquad (3.6)$$

where the number of trained patterns w replaces z because $w \cong p_T z$, and $1/p_T$ appears in the second factor of Equation (3.1), as detailed below. $p_T = w/z$ is normally vanishingly small because $z \cong 2^{S_o}$ where the number of synapses S_o in neocortical neurons typically exceeds 1000.

This derivation assumed that the sequence in which patterns are taught is irrelevant, which is strictly true on physical grounds for the synapse atrophy (SA) model mentioned above and simulated in Section 3.2, for which all synapse strengths remain equal to one throughout training and only their mortality changes after all training ends. The pattern sequence does not matter during recall because synapse strength is no longer plastic then. Also, if only a vanishing fraction w/z of z possible patterns is taught, then the assumption in Equation (3.1) that mutual information is approximately additive is valid; note that L in Equation (3.6) is proportional to $w \ll z$, not to z.

When synapse strengths change during learning, as assumed for the CB and CE synapse strength (SS) models, the probabilities in Equation (3.1) become time dependent. However, this mild time dependence does not materially affect L for the following reasons. When a pattern is learned its associated synapses gain strength, thus slightly increasing the learning probability for subsequently taught patterns that use those same synapses. Consequently new learned patterns will tend to slightly resemble the cumulative ensemble previously learned so that the effective number of fully independent patterns will be less than z.

Since the sum in Equation 3.1 is approximately proportional to the ratio w/z, as derived below, therefore only w matters in Equation 3.6 and any reduction in z due to pattern correlations becomes largely irrelevant. The probability of confusion among the $p_L w$ learned patterns remains negligible compared to p_F because $w \ll z$ and because the patterns are individually quite sparse. Thus any correlations among the w patterns are largely irrelevant so long as they are sufficiently distinct when being recognized. Sparseness means that patterns have relatively few 1's, which implies that the neuron firing threshold is small compared to the number of synapses.

As noted earlier, Equation 3.6 yields an important conclusion: no information L is recoverable unless $p_F < p_L$, which implies that the neuron must change state in some way between its nascent learning phase and its mature testing phase, as it does in both the SS (the threshold H increases during recall) and SA (unused synapses atrophy before recall) learning models. Otherwise, if synapse strength is time invariant, both Alice and Bob will observe that the same fraction $p_L \cong p_F$ of all z patterns excites an output, yielding $L = 0$. If learning increases synapse strengths so as to increase p_L as more patterns are learned, then the initial value of p_L applies to the requirement $p_F < p_L$. A more complete version of this derivation appears in Appendix B.

Equation 3.6 is therefore a very important result because it shows that if a spike signifies only that the responsible excitation pattern had been seen during training, then a learning-ready neuron must either: 1) raise its firing threshold, 2) reduce all spike amplitudes, 3) eliminate some little used synapses, or 4) do something equivalent before useful information can be extracted.

3.3 Simulations of the cognon extended (CE) model

Because the CE model now has more degrees of freedom, exploration of all possible variants would be tedious. Therefore, only approximate optimizations of L are presented here, with and without the assumption of homology (constancy across multiple neural layers) in neural firing rates R or numbers of delays D, as explained later.

For convenience Table 3.1 summarizes definitions of the parameters used in the following discussions.

The first question involves how well the CE neuron model performs when the numbers of independent dendrite compartments C and available inter-pattern delays D exceed one. Table 3.2 shows time-domain simulator input parameters and output results for neurons with 10,000, 1000, and 200 synapses. Each row of the table corresponds to a different set of the

Table 3.1. Summary definitions of neural parameters

Parameter	Definition
C	Number of dendrite compartments capable of firing independently
D	Number of possible time slots where neurons can produce spikes
D'	Number of different time delays available between two neural layers
D_{eff}	D for a boxcar delay distribution that has entropy = output-distribution entropy
G	High/low ratios for both the synapse strength S_i and the firing threshold H during training
H	Firing threshold per compartment = required number of excited synapses of strength 1
L	Maximum retrievable information per neuron (bits), $I[\overline{X},\overline{Y}]$ *
p_F	Probability that a mature neuron will fire for an untrained pattern
p_L	Probability of learning a random pattern presented during plasticity and learning readiness
p_R	Probability that a synapse will ever be strengthened; $p_R = E[S_m/S_o]$*
p_T	Probability that a random pattern in Z would be presented during training
R	Average number of patterns per afferent synapse spike; $R = 1/p_L$ for homology
S_o	Initial number of synapses per neuron
S_m	Number of maximum-strength synapses after plasticity ends
T	Period of spike waves (say ~30 msec in nature; perhaps γ^{-1})
w	Number of patterns (words) taught (presented during plasticity and readiness)
W	The value of w that maximizes $L = I[\overline{X},\overline{Y}]$ *
z,Z	Number or set of possible mature input patterns

* E[ ] is the expectation operator and $I[\overline{X},\overline{Y}]$ is the mutual information between the vectors $\overline{X}$ and $\overline{Y}$.

neuron input parameters S_o, C, and D. The results include several performance parameters averaged over multiple neuron trials for combinations of the variables R, G, H, and w that were independently optimized for each row of the table. The table entries are grouped by their values of D and C, and in declining order of bits/neuron, which ranges between 1623 and 23. For the best listed cases the parameter bits/synapse

Table 3.2. Maximized values of L (bits/neuron) as a function of the CE model parameters

C	D	S_o	L	H	R	G	p_F(%)	p_L	w	S_G/S_o
10	4	10,000	1632	5	125	1.8	0.79	0.24	2000	0.26
1	4	10,000	1052	5	384	3.8	1.2	0.58	400	0.15
4	4	10,000	893	5	178	3.2	0.2	0.36	500	0.16
10	1	10,000	812	5	333	3.8	2.6	0.88	200	0.24
4	1	10,000	808	10	357	3.6	0.65	0.53	300	0.36
1	1	10,000	713	30	303	4.0	1.2	0.72	200	0.48
1	1	1000	157	5	285	4.0	2.0	0.28	200	0.36
4	4	1000	148	5	25	1.9	1.7	0.25	200	0.26
1	4	1000	146	5	83	1.9	1.4	0.14	500	0.35
4	1	1000	130	5	83	3.8	2.7	0.57	60	0.29
10	4	1000	121	5	10	1.8	2.5	0.48	70	0.18
1	1	200	33	5	57	3.8	2.4*	0.29	40	0.36
1	4	200	28	5	16	1.8	1.8*	0.15	80	0.31
4	1	200	23	5	16	3.8	4.5*	0.61	10	0.26
4	4	200	23	5	5	1.9	3.7*	0.23	40	0.24

*p_F rms > 0.5 p_F

ranges between 0.07 and 0.16 for S_o = 10,000 synapses, between 0.12 and 0.16 for S_o = 1000 synapses, and between 0.06 and 0.16 for S_o = 200 synapses. In each case where D = 4, we assumed D' = 7 so as to ensure $D_{eff} \cong D$ and that D would not increase unduly after signals propagate through several neural layers.

Each trial was optimized by automatic searching of all given combinations of input parameters where R was any integer up to 400, G was between 1 and 2 spaced at 0.1 and between 2 and 4 spaced at 0.2, H was between 5 and 250 spaced at 5, and w was spaced at 10 for values between 10 and 100, spaced at 100 for values up to 1000, and spaced at 1000 for values up to 10,000. The resulting false alarm and learning probabilities p_F and p_L are also listed, along with the number w of patterns presented during learning readiness and the fraction S_G/S_o of strong synapses that result after learning is optimized and ceases.

The main result of Table 3.2 is that the CE model, despite its simplicity concerning neuron function (adequately characterized by H, R, D, and C) and the simplicity of information extraction (spikes signify only that the current excitation pattern was probably seen during learning readiness), nonetheless the recoverable Shannon information stored per synapse, L/S_o bits/synapse, exceeds 0.1 for most neuron configurations that are consistent with fast learning and recall. As noted earlier this performance is competitive with that predicted for other models employing quite different assumptions despite the simplicity of the cognon models.

The table also suggests why evolution might favor utilization of compartments ($C > 1$) and diversity in intra-pattern delay ($D > 1$); they allow the product $R \cdot H$ to assume much lower values for the largest neurons, large neurons being able to recall more patterns of greater complexity. The product $R \cdot H$ is important because the random firing of $\sim S_o/RCD$ inputs for each pattern summation should not exceed H, which would produce a false alarm. That is, we want $S_o > HRCD$, which it is for every entry in Table 3.2 except the second line. For most lines $HRCD \cong 1.5\ S_o$. The formula S_o/RCD arises because of the S_o potential inputs to a summation, only S_o/RCD are likely to be summed for a single pattern within one of C compartments and one of D time slots.

The exception on the second line is probably due to the fact that $D_{eff} \cong 6$, not 4, so using D_{eff} instead of D in the formula, which is more appropriate, eliminates the exception. In fact, $D_{eff} \cong 6$ for most table entries with $D = 4$. If there were no increase in delay dispersion so that $D_{eff} \cong D$, then L would be reduced slightly.

Reducing R (average number of excitation patterns received per spike produced) is biologically important because it controls the response speed of a neural network, which has survival value. For example, if R exceeds 30 for patterns arriving at a gamma wave frequency of 30 Hz, then the average input neuron would spike less than once per second, which could slow animal response times.

The alternative evolutionary solution of increasing H may become metabolically expensive if the total cost of synapses on a neuron exceeds the metabolic cost of the cell body, as suggested later in the discussion of the Table 3.5 results. That is, evolution of compartments and differential spike timing within patterns could be motivated by the computational rewards of using neurons with more synapses while retaining swift reactions and limiting metabolic costs.

The table also suggests that the fraction S_G/S_o of strong synapses varies between 0.1 and 0.6, depending on C, D, and other parameters. If synapse strength distributions can be measured and related to these parameters, this would provide another way to validate cognon models as potential guides to neural behavior.

Finally, Table 3.2 suggests that G should be between 1.6 and 4, with 3.8-4 being preferred for maximum values of L; the cases where $G > 4$ were not examined. However, as shown earlier in Tables 2.1, 2.3, and 2.4, and soon by Table 3.4, lower values of G also work well.

The potential benefits of $C > 1$, $D > 1$ can also be evaluated under the constraining assumption of homology in both parameters. Homology in R was explained earlier; it simply requires that the average firing rate of a neuron during learning (p_L during learning) or recall ($1/R$) approximate the average firing rate ($1/R$) of its input neurons, i..e., $p_L \cdot R \cong 1$. Partial homology requires that this product merely be reasonably bounded. For example, the simulations in Table 3.2 examined several cases where $1 < p_L \cdot R < 10$ that generally store more information than when $p_L \cdot R \cong 1$.

Homology in D requires that the time span of a slightly time-dispersed pattern remains approximately constant as the pattern propagates from layer to layer. That is, the number D of resolvable time slots occupied by spikes belonging to a particular pattern should not systematically increase layer to layer, or presumably beyond the bounds set by inter-pattern separations, say 25 milliseconds for gamma waves. D would therefore probably be limited to values below 8, say, if the time resolution of spike synchrony were roughly 2 milliseconds. Slower waves or asynchronous single "overspread" patterns spanning more than one EEG period might permit larger values. Whether overspread patterns with excessive D values could be processed correctly is unknown; this issue is not explored here.

Since the probability distribution of the output neuron model spike emissions represents the convolution of the delay distribution of the input excitory spikes from the preceding layer, and the additional delays introduced in the axon/synapse/dendrite propagation path prior to summation, one might suspect that the output delay distribution would spread layer to layer uncontrollably. However, that does not generally happen because statistically those spikes that arrive for summation early or late are relatively rare and typically cannot sum to meet the threshold; the central time slots are heavily favored, as explained later in this section. The metric used to characterize the width of the output spike distribution, D_{eff}, was arbitrarily chosen as the width of a uniform boxcar delay distribution that has the same entropy as the output spike delay distribution from the model neuron. $D_{eff} = 1$ if $D = 1$.

The net effect of adding multiple dendrite compartments and inter-pattern delays, C and D, to the CB model is significant because the number of patterns that it can then learn for given values of R and H increases markedly. We find for SA learning models limited by homology in R and D that the optimum numbers of synapses S_o that result from arguably plausible values of C, D, R, and H can then exceed 10,000 or more, as observed in nature. One might therefore preferentially seek such compartmented and delay-sensitive behavior in cortical neurons known to have many synapses and significant memory duties.

One reason the number of patterns recognized by a single model neuron increases as C and D increase is that the patterns tested against the threshold H become increasingly sparse and therefore orthogonal because patterns then have a lower fraction of spikes (1's), and the patterns can increase in length. The average number of time-synchronous spikes per pattern or dendrite compartment remains in the neighborhood of H, however. These consequences are apparent in the simulation results.

To compare the performance of SS and SA learning we simulated in the time domain neural models characterized by a wide range of given values of H, R, D, and C. Each excitation pattern was characterized by which synapses i were excited and at which afferent soma delays D_i. For each output model neuron D_i was independently and identically distributed

(IID) over D possibilities. The probability that a given afferent output soma was excited during any particular pattern was R^{-1}.

L was maximized for each modeled combination of H, R, D, and C, first by choosing S_o and D' to ensure that the mean output firing rate R and delay spread D were comparable to those at the neural inputs. Otherwise R and D would increase rapidly across successive neural layers (L increases with R and D). Then the values of w and G that maximize L were found; these steps were manually iterated for the results presented below.

The delay spread D' within a neural unit arises from some combination of axon propagation and synapse/dendrite response times, which could be ~20 msec (Gollisch & Meister, 2008; Rall, 1977; Branco, Clark, & Hausser, 2010), consistent with the range of spike delays observed following a flashed retinal image. The resulting values for L and other parameters for eight diverse optimized SA and SS neural models are listed in Table 3.3A and 3.3B, respectively; abbreviations are defined in Table 3.1. The second through seventh synapse strength (SS) parameter sets were also tested for synapse atrophy (SA), permitting comparisons.

Several conclusions can be drawn from Table 3.3. First, synapse atrophy (SA) learning permits storage of roughly 2-7 times as much information L per neuron as does synapse-strength (SS) learning for these examples, and roughly 1.5-5 times as much information storage per stronger synapse, L/S_m. For example, $L_{SA}/L_{SS} \cong 2$ for the $[D,C,H,R] = [1, 10, 10, 30]$ case, and $L_{SA}/L_{SS} \cong 7$ for the [4, 1, 30, 30] case. Also it is clear that neither delay diversity ($D > 1$) nor compartments ($C > 1$) are necessary for useful performance, although they do permit lower values of R for high performance using fixed values of S_o. Lower values of R correspond to more frequent spiking and therefore greater data rates. For this diverse set of models the bits per synapse (L/S_m) range 0.02-0.3, roughly consistent with typical prior estimates (Baldassi et al., 2007; Barrett & van Rossum, 2008).

Second, the performance of SS models is not heavily dependent on the ratio G, as illustrated for the [1, 1, 30, 30] case where the maximum L varies less than a factor of two as G varies from 1.2 to 2.0. For the remaining SS cases only the results for the approximately optimum G are shown. These optimum G values are generally higher for the simpler neural models, which yield lower values of L. This may result partly because the relative standard deviations in the excitation sums are higher in simpler models where fewer random events are added, and higher values of G can better accommodate this increased variation.

Table 3.3. Illustrative time-domain simulation results comparing the SS and SA CE models when L (bits/neuron) is manually maximized subject to homology in spike frequency ($p_L R \cong 1$) and spike time dispersion ($D \cong D_{\mathit{eff}}$).

Model parameters   Average results

D	C	H	R	G	L	L/S_m	30L/W	S_m	Wp_L	p_F	L/Wp_L	S_o	W	D'
					b/n*	mb/syn	b/s/n	#/n	#/n	%	b/w	#/n	w/n	#
A. SA Learning														
1	1	10	10	-	11.6	360	8.7	32.2	4.1	0.34	2.8	64	40	1
1	1	30	30	-	47.8	100	1.55	489	31	0.22	1.54	626	925	1
1	10	10	10	-	34.8	250	5.96	139	19	1.01	1.8	421	175	1
1	10	10	30	-	102	220	1.61	454	62	0.17	1.6	1056	1900	1
1	10	30	30	-	257	100	1.93	2633	130	0.06	2.0	5184	4000	1
4	1	30	30	-	307	120	1.94	2627	161	0.10	1.9	3888	4750	7
4	1	100	30	-	529	40	1.72	13019	311	0.16	1.7	16344	9200	7
8	4	20	20	-	1232	200	3.70	6164	513	0.12	2.4	10542	10000	14
B. SS Learning														
1	1	30	30	1.2	6.6	44	1.3	152	5.1	0.34	1.31	654	150	1
1	1	30	30	1.6	7.5	43	2.2	172	3.3	0.01	2.24	621	100	1
1	1	30	30	2.0	5.1	19	1.5	275	3.2	0.18	1.59	626	100	1
1	10	10	10	1.6	6.8	50	5.1	119	4.0	1.10	1.70	520	40	1
1	10	10	30	1.3	52	146	1.4	359	37	0.28	1.42	1086	1100	1
1	10	30	30	1.2	74	45	1.9	1625	48	0.23	1.54	5238	1400	1
4	1	30	30	1.2	44	29	1.0	1522	43	0.50	1.01	3888	1300	7
4	10	30	30	1.2	424	39	1.4	11012	296	0.25	1.43	33030	9000	7

* Abbreviations: b = bits, mb = millibits, n = neuron, syn = synapse, s = second, w = pattern, # = number

Third, the optimum numbers of naïve (S_o) and mature (S_m) synapses can exceed 10,000 for larger neural models (e.g., [SA: 4,1,100,30] and [SS: 4,10,30,30], consistent with neurological observations despite their tenuous link with these simple models (Koch, 1999). To the extent these models suggest real neural behavior, the implication is that neurons with tens of thousands of synapses may employ effectively compartmented and more heavily branched dendrites, or may discriminate between excitation patterns for which $D > 1$.

Fourth, it appears from the approximate upper bound $30L/W$ (bits/sec) listed in the table that information can be extracted fairly rapidly at rates differing less than a factor of two between comparable SA and SS model neurons; this estimate assumes an average pattern presentation rate of 30 Hz. This rough bound equals the bits per pattern learned (L/Wp_L) times the rate at which learned patterns might be presented. If we assume a test excitation-pattern ensemble similar to that applied when the model was learning, then if 30 such patterns were presented per second, of these patterns only $30/R$ would have been learned. Since $p_L R \cong 1$ if the input and output spiking rates R are to be comparable, the upper bound becomes $30L/W$ bits/sec. By comparing this rate bound to L it appears these models can plausibly release most of their information content within the time $W/30$, or within seconds to minutes, depending on their information content and the set of excitations patterns used to extract it.

Rapid extraction requires that only the most environmentally relevant patterns sensed by a particular neuron are presented, not noise. The table also suggests that hundreds of patterns ($W \cdot p_L$) can be learned by each SA neuron, several times more than by SS neurons having similar parameters, and that the bits per pattern learned (or per spike) L/Wp_L range between 1 and 3 for all models, similar to prior suggestions, (e.g., Rieke et al., 1996).

Fifth, for optimum recall performance the spontaneous false-alarm rates (p_F) per pattern are on the order of 0.1-1 percent, corresponding to a false alarm every few seconds if we again assume a 30-Hz pattern presentation rate. This implies that neural malfunctions promoting random firing at rates higher than this are likely to degrade performance. It also suggests the possibility that most observed spikes may be important and that observed correlations over ensembles are probably missing most of the underlying information being communicated; this is particularly true if only a fraction of each neuron's inputs are monitored.

Sixth, if there is delay dispersion within patterns ($D > 1$), then the modeled delay dispersion D' within neurons exceeds D by nearly a factor of two for all models, assuming the delay dispersion remains roughly constant from one neural layer to the next. This non-obvious result may be explained by the fact that if both the spike and neural delay distributions were equal-length uniform boxcars, then the total delay distribution would be their convolution, or a triangle that would strongly favor spike generation near the triangle's peak, thus significantly diminishing D at the neural output. Nominal equality of D at both input and output therefore generally requires that $D' > D$ if $D > 1$.

For boxcar spike arrival distributions we found $D' \cong 2D - 1$ using simulations, which is consistent with the convolution of two boxcar widths (D and D') to yield a trapezoid with a maximum length at the top near D. Since only afferent neurons that produce net delays near the top of the probability trapezoid are likely to be incorporated in patterns that are learned, the effective R for afferent neurons contributing to the ramps of the trapezoid is therefore increased to $R' \cong R(2D-1)/D$. More realistic delay distributions for excitation spikes would round the corners of the theoretical trapezoid, further lowering the success probability of spikes and therefore their energy efficiency, measured as Joules per bit or spike; thus the simulations in Table 3.2 are slightly optimistic for this reason.

Finally, these results suggest that a hybrid learning strategy that combines the high-L benefits of the SA model with the learning flexibility of the SS model may be superior to SA or SS learning alone. For example, most neurons might frequently shift between their learning and recall modes using SS learning until w approaches values where L peaks, and then some of the older, less utilized synapses might atrophy so that new synapses with strength $s_i = 1$ could be added and trained. This process could continually iterate as the neuron slowly grows larger over its lifespan. Although it is well known that less useful synapses atrophy and that firing thresholds vary, the relationship between such behavior and recall skill has not been well measured in nature (Koch, 1999).

Each experiment averaged the performance of at least 10 neurons, each of which was tested on roughly 100,000 randomly chosen excitation patterns. Small variations in the results occur because: 1) of finite averaging, 2) D, D', and H are integers, and 3) these optimizations employed manual multi-dimensional hill-climbing; these three error sources appear to be roughly comparable.

The values of C, D, D', H, and R, used in these simulations are arguably consistent with nature. The number of C independent dendrite compartments is likely to be unity or related to the number of major dendrite branches closely coupled to the soma, perhaps no more than 15, depending on neural type. The delay spread D' within a neural unit arises from some combination of axon propagation and synapse/dendrite response times, which could be ~20 msec, consistent with observed relation times and the range of spike delays observed following a flashed retinal image (Gollisch & Meister, 2008; Rall, 1977; Branco, Clark, & Hausser, 2010). A rough upper limit to D' is therefore perhaps (20 msec)/(2 msec) = 10, assuming spike widths and coincidences of ~2 msec. If homology applies and $D' \cong 2D - 1$, then D might lie between unity and 6.

As noted earlier, the threshold H probably lies between ~60, a nominal ratio of threshold-to-single-spike voltages, and ~9, a nominal ratio of threshold-to-single-spike currents. Since these threshold-to-single-spike ratios may be misleading if post-synaptic effects superimpose non-linearly, as some evidence suggests (London & Hausser, 2005; Rall, 1977), we explore H values as low as 5, where low values often yield the highest values for bits/synapse. We can infer that R lies roughly between 4 and 40 if the period T between spike waves (patterns presented) approximates that for gamma waves, say 25 msec, and the observed intervals between consecutive spikes for attentive animals are ~100-1000 msec.

Table 3.4 presents a lengthier set of results for the synapse atrophy (SA) model where S_o and w were manually optimized to maximize the information stored per neuron (L bits) for the given model parameters D, C, H, and R while satisfying homology for R and D. Hereafter "word" is often used interchangeably with "pattern." Listed parameters of interest also include averages of the: 1) bits stored per mature synapse L/S_m, 2) bits/second, $\gamma L/W$, that a neuron could communicate when the spike-wave pattern frequency $\gamma = 30$ Hz, 3) optimum number of mature synapses S_m, 4) maximum number of words learned Wp_L, 5) false-alarm probability p_F for an optimized mature neuron, 6) bits stored per word learned L/Wp_L, 7) optimum number S_o of naïve synapses, 8) optimum number W of words taught, 9) delay spread D' introduced by the afferent axon/synapse/dendrite system, 10) entropy D_{eff} of the output delay spread, which equals D under homology, and 11) metric $p_L R$ for achievement of homology in spike frequency; $p_L R$ should approximate unity. **Boldface** entries are maxima or minima for that column.

Table 3.4. Time-domain simulation results for the synapse atrophy learning model (SA) constrained by homology

Model parameters   Average results

D	C	H	R	L	L/S_m	30L/W	S_m	Wp_L	p_F	L/Wp_L	S_o	W	D'	D_eff	Rp_L
				b/n*	b/syn	b/s/n	#/n	#/n	%	b/w	#/n	w/n	#	#	-
1	1	10	10	12	0.36	8.7	**32.2**	**4.1**	0.34	2.8	**64**	40	1	1	1.04
1	1	10	30	22	0.25	1.9	87.5	12	0.13	1.8	153	350	1	1	1.04
1	1	30	10	24	0.16	10	148	7.3	0.17	**3.3**	236	70	1	1	1.05
1	1	30	30	48	0.10	1.6	489	31	0.22	1.5	626	925	1	1	1.00
1	4	5	20	17	**0.46**	2.9	37.2	9.1	0.30	1.9	111	180	1	1	1.01
1	4	20	5	14	0.12	**11**	114	8.1	**2.48**	1.7	270	40	1	1	1.01
1	10	10	10	35	0.25	6.0	139	19	1.01	1.8	421	175	1	1	1.06
1	10	10	30	102	0.22	**1.6**	454	62	0.17	**1.6**	1056	1900	1	1	0.98
1	10	30	10	82	0.10	6.6	784	39	0.74	2.1	1890	375	1	1	1.05
1	10	30	30	257	0.10	1.9	2633	130	0.06	2.0	5184	4000	1	1	0.98
1	20	20	20	230	0.14	2.8	1697	124	0.30	1.8	3904	2500	1	1	0.99
2	4	20	20	234	0.15	2.5	1587	137	0.36	1.7	2546	2800	3	2.0	0.98
4	1	10	10	59	0.38	8.8	152	21	0.33	2.8	301	200	6	4.2	1.04
4	1	10	30	111	0.25	1.7	443	68	0.20	1.6	749	2000	6	3.9	1.03
4	1	30	10	149	0.17	9.4	890	50	0.28	3.0	1425	475	7	4.3	1.06
4	1	30	30	307	0.12	1.9	2627	161	**0.10**	1.9	3888	4750	7	4.2	1.01
4	1	100	10	267	0.06	9.4	4129	84	0.17	3.2	5710	850	7	4.0	0.99
4	1	100	30	529	**0.04**	1.7	**13019**	311	0.16	1.7	**16344**	9200	7	4.0	1.01
8	4	20	20	**1232**	0.20	3.7	6164	**513**	0.12	2.4	10542	**10000**	14	8.4	1.03

* Abbreviations: b = bits, n = neuron, syn = synapse, s = second, w = word (pattern), # = number

The SA simulator results in Table 3.4 were fitted to simple polynomials presented in Table 3.5 that predict performance parameters. The indicated rms accuracies in the table are the linearized equivalents of the rms discrepancies found in logarithmic space. More elaborate polynomials would fit the data better, but the rudimentary conclusions we seek would not seem to warrant the effort given the small number of simulations.

Table 3.5 Polynomial approximations to optimized SA model-neuron parameters

Parameter	Approximate polynomial		Simplified approximation
L	$0.23\, D^{1.35} R^{0.86} C^{0.67} H^{0.72}$	±24%	$0.3\, (D^2RCH)^{0.7}$ (bits/neuron)
L/S_m	$3.3\, D^{0.11} R^{-0.2} C^{-0.08} H^{0.81}$	± 13%	$3\, R^{-0.2} H^{0.8}$ (bits/mature synapse)
L/Wp_L	$4.7\, D^{0.05} R^{-0.3} C^{-0.06} H^{0.02}$	± 16%	2 (bits/pattern learned; bits/spike)
S_m	$0.34\, D^{1.2} R^{0.87} C^{0.88} H^{1.35}$	± 10%	$0.3\, (DH)^{1.3}(RC)^{0.9}$ (naïve synapses/neuron)
S_m/S_o	$0.20\, D^{0.03} R^{0.19} C^{-0.13} H^{0.18}$	± 9%	$0.2(RH/C)^{1/6} \cong 50\%$ (reinforcement prob.)
Wp_L	$0.049\, D^{1.29} R^{1.15} C^{0.73} H^{0.69}$	± 19%	$0.05\, (DR)^{1.2}(CH)^{0.7}$ (patterns learned)
S_m/p_LW	$1.41\, D^{-0.06} R^{-0.09} C^{0.02} H^{0.83}$	± 5%	$H^{0.8}$ (mature synapses/pattern learned)
p_F	$0.076\, D^{-0.13} R^{-1.04} C^{0.14} H^{0.18}$	± 61%	$0.07\, R^{-1}$ (false alarm probability)
$\gamma L/W$	$5.4\gamma\, D^{0.06} R^{-1.33} C^{-0.07} H^{0.01}$	± 11%	$5\gamma\, R^{-1.3}$ (bits/neuron/second)

The first result of interest involves the ability of SA neurons and synapses to store bits and memorize patterns. The first polynomial in Table 3.5 is an approximate upper bound to memory capacity L for an SA neuron. The associated simplified expression for L (bits/neuron) is $\sim 0.3(D^2RCH)^{0.7}$, which can be very roughly interpreted. Its four factors can be viewed as semi-orthogonal dimensions of a space in which bits can be placed. Recall that any SA compartment must have approximately $R \cdot H$

synapses in order to fire with reasonable probability, corresponding to a maximum of 2^{RH} possible messages and $\log_2(2^{RH}) = R \cdot H$ bits for one message if they are equiprobable.

This reasoning leads to an approximate upper bound to L of $R \cdot H$ bits in each of C compartments for each of D delays (yields $\sim RHCD$ bits). However, each synapse in each compartment can fire in $\sim D$ possible time slots, offering $(RH)^D$ combinations or $D\log_2(RH)$ which adds to the $RHCD$ bits. A small increase in the D dependence therefore seems plausible, perhaps approximating D^2RHC and the simulation results for L, which are evidently diminished by learning and recall inefficiencies to $\sim 0.3(D^2RCH)^{0.7}$. Although this derivation is rough it does provide some intuition.

The efficiency of such storage is also suggested by the memory capacity of mature SA synapses, L/S_m (bits/mature synapse), which approximates $3R^{-0.2}H^{-0.8}$ for the assumed range of model neural parameters listed in Table 3.4. Over this range, L/S_m varies between 0.04 and 0.46 bits/mature-synapse and averages 0.19, which is consistent with prior estimates (Baldassi, Braunstein, Brunel, & Zecchina, 2007; Barrett & van Rossum, 2008). Most such prior models assume that both learning/forgetting and synapse strength vary slowly over multiple learning events. An early exception was the multi-neuron instant learning model for an associative memory inspired by holography (Willshaw, Buneman, & Longuet-Higgins, 1969) and discussed in Section 2.6.

Related questions involve the maximum numbers of bits conveyed per spike or stored within a typical synapse, and which factors determine the optimum value of H. Table 3.5 provides the interesting result that each of the $w \cdot p_L$ learned patterns yields $L/wp_L \cong 2$ bits. If we extract this information efficiently by testing for all w learned patterns and all are recognized, then we might conclude each recognition spike conveyed two bits of information, consistent with prior estimates (Rieke, Warland, van Steveninck, & Bialek, 1996). The metric bits/spike is proportional to the survival-relevant metric, bits/Joule, and therefore one of the parameters probably maximized by evolution.

Since $L/S_m \propto H^{-0.8}$, which favors low values of H if synapses are metabolically expensive, and $L \propto H^{0.7}$, which favors large H if neural cell bodies are relatively more expensive, it follows that the optimum value of H is partly determined by the relative metabolic costs of neural cell bodies versus those of synapses. In contrast, the other survival-relevant metrics of bits/spike and bits/neuron/second are nearly independent of H.

Another test for any neural model is its ability to explain why neurons have so many synapses. Both the last two entries in Table 3.4 and the polynomials for S_o and S_m in Table 3.5 show that larger neural models can advantageously utilize more than 10,000 synapses, and perhaps even 100,000. Since neocortical pyramidal cells can have ~10,000 afferent synapses, and Purkinje cells in the cerebellum may have 200,000 (Koch, 1999), in order for these cells to be both memory-optimum and consistent with these SA model results they probably employ more than one resolvable delay ($D > 1$) and the equivalent of multiple dendrite compartments ($C > 1$), assuming that biology limits the polynomial factor $R^{0.8}H^{1.3} < \sim 10,000$.

It would therefore be interesting to compare estimated *in vivo* [D, R, C, H, S_o] combinations for different cell types with SA predictions of which combinations are more nearly optimum with respect to utility metrics such as L, L/S_m, $\gamma L/W$, and total metabolic cost. Similar comparisons with polynomials derived for the synapse strength (SS) model would also be interesting, although Table 3.2 suggests that the information storage L and other parameters would be somewhat lower than for the SA learning model.

The simulation-based polynomial for p_F in Table 3.5 suggests that at maturity the optimum SA homologous false-alarm probability $p_F \cong 0.07 \, p_L$ (since $R^{-1} = p_L$) and that it ranges from 0.06 to 2.5 percent for the cases listed in Table 3.4. Thus such memory should remain functional when burdened by random firing at comparable levels (say ~0.1-0.4 spikes/sec), which is not very demanding. The converse implication is also interesting; all non-random spikes may have very precise meanings, and small perturbations in their timing or propagation success may reduce performance significantly below the bounds estimated here. Some of this could be compensated by the fact that these neural models are far simpler than real neurons.

A metric other than memory that promotes organism survival is the rate (bits/sec/neuron) at which a neuron can transmit its information. This rate roughly equals the average bits per spike L/Wp_L times the average number of spikes per second, γ/R, where γ is the nominal pattern frequency [Hz]; $(L/Wp_L)(\gamma/R) = \gamma L/W$. Table 3.5 suggests that $\gamma L/W \cong 5\gamma/R^{1.3}$, which motivates small values of R rather than large values that maximize L, a competing survival metric. Survival might therefore be optimized by intermediate values of R that serve both information rate and memory survival objectives reasonably well. This also suggests that cortical regions with high average R may be more memory intensive, while those with low R values may be more time critical.

Although the variables $RHCD$ have been regarded here as arbitrary inputs, they may have natural optima determined by cost functions that depend, for example, on survival objectives in the case of R and on the relative metabolic costs of synapses versus neurons in the case of H, as suggested earlier; other costs may also enter. Large values for C imply large numbers of synapses with attendant metabolic costs and may also challenge the branching architecture of dendrite arbors. Similarly the significant advantages of high D values are presumably balanced by biological limits to spike time resolution and timing stability, and by the desire for rapid cognitive responses that require high-frequency spike-wave patterns. Therefore such organism optimization issues provide another avenue for testing the relevance of such extended neural models to real neurons and real organisms.

3.4. Extended cognon time-domain simulator

The simulator is written in C++ and operates in a Linux environment. More detailed source code explanations, listings, and instructions for downloading the complete sources and data are provided in Appendix B.

The CB neuron learning simulator trains and tests an ensemble of neurons having given parameters and reports the average results for various parameters, particularly the mean and standard deviation for the probability of learning p_L, probability of false alarms p_F, and learned information metric L. The simulator accumulates a wide variety of other statistics, such as the number of synapses strengthened during training, which are available through the programmatic interface.

To collect sufficient and sufficiently accurate statistics for the probability of learning, the system trains enough neurons so that at least 10,000 words are exposed to neurons during training in aggregate across the ensemble. For example, if each neuron were exposed to ten words during training, then the system would train 1000 neurons. In any event, at least ten neurons are trained, no matter how many words are in the training set for each neuron.

To collect sufficient statistics for the probability of false alarms, each neuron configuration is tested, over its ensemble, on a total of at least 1,000,000 random words that do not belong to the training set. The number of random words on which each neuron is tested depends on the number of neurons in the ensemble, but in any event no neuron is ever tested on fewer than 1000 random words. For many variables the accuracy of the resulting average is represented by the standard deviations of the M samples relative to their mean, divided by $\sqrt{M-1}$.

In general the simulator may be given a neuron configuration, usually specified as some combination of C, D, D', H, R, S_o, G, and w, and it reports the various statistics of interest for that specific configuration; these include the average values and standard deviations of L, p_F, and p_L, and other results such as S_o/L, S_m and L/w. There are provisions in the system to report the data in a comma-separated-value (CSV) format suitable for input to a spreadsheet or other data processing system. Within the simulator code and output data slightly different names are used for some variables: $D \to D1$, $D' \to D2$, $S_o \to S$, $w \to W$, and $Q = S_o/(H \cdot R \cdot C)$. All inputs and outputs are displayed on an Excel spreadsheet, where each line represents the average of many single-neuron experiments.

The large number of configuration parameters means that a very large high-dimensional parameter space must be searched when seeking optimal performance. To generate data for some tables, particularly Tables 2.3 and 3.3, we developed a simple heuristic search algorithm that is given a partial configuration of *H, S, C, D1,* and *D2*, with parameters describing the grid search parameters for *G*, and that seeks local optimum performance by doing a grid search on *W, Q, R,* and *G* with early stopping. *W* was restricted to one of the values {10, 20, 30, ..., 90, 100, 200, 300, ..., 900, 1000, 2000, ..., 10,000}. *Q* was any number in the range {0.5, 2·*D1*}. *R* was an integer constrained to the range {2, ..., 400}. *G* was constrained to be in the range from *G_max* down to one, quantized by *G_step* increments. *H_m* was defined as *H·G*, although other untested choices might perform slightly better. *G_max*, and *G_step* were chosen to be plausibly consistent with neurological parameters and vary from experiment to experiment.

The CB time-domain neuron simulator uses two key classes of variables: neurons and words. Each neuron has S_o synapses, each of which has a strength value that is equal to either unity or *G* prior to being exposed to each new word vector. Initially all synapses have strength one. A word, which defines an excitation pattern, contains a list of those input synapses that fired for the most recent given excitation pattern, and a single neuron matrix corresponds to a chronological list of words, one per excitation pattern presented to that neuron.

The two main routines are "train" and "expose." To train a neuron, "train" is called for each word to be recognized. If the neuron fires for that word then all synapses that contributed to that firing have their strengths irreversibly increased to *G*. Once training is complete the neuron's threshold value *H* is set to *H·G* by the external code, which also hosts the neuron model parameters *R* and *w*, where 1/*R* is defined as the fraction of the words for which each synapse independently fires, and *w* is the number of words to be exposed to the neuron during training.

The routine "expose" models how the neuron reacts to excitation patterns, and how it computes whether or not to fire. This is embedded within an envelope that calls this code. Expose computes the weighted sum of the input word, and the neuron fires if that sum meets or exceeds a threshold. The weighted sum is the sum of the S_o element-by-element products of the most recent neuron vector, and the current word. The firing threshold is increased slightly by "epsilon" to avoid effects of rounding and representational errors in floating point arithmetic. A more detailed description of the simulator is presented in Appendix B.

This CE model simulator accommodates the CB model by simply setting the input parameters C = D = 1. The neuron simulator is written in C++, uses the standard template library (STL), and typically operates in a Linux environment. For performance it may use OpenMP to compute various simulations in parallel. The full simulator and its source code are available for download from *http://cognon.net*. Suggestions for its use and a more complete description appear in Appendix B.

Chapter 4
Relationship between the extended neuron learning models and neuroscience

4.1   Summary of the key results of Chapters 2 and 3

It is useful to summarize the key results of the preceding chapters before linking them to neuroscience:

1) Simulations have demonstrated that a simple threshold-firing binary CB model can learn a new pattern in less than a second and subsequently fire in the same time with certainty when re-exposed to any excitation pattern that it previously learned.

2) A pattern is learned when those plastic synapses that contributed to an output spike are modestly strengthened while the neuron firing threshold was temporarily lowered from $G \cdot H$ to H and the neuron was therefore temporarily learning ready. For convenience and plausibility both the fraction of input neurons that fire for a given pattern, and the fraction of patterns exposed to the neuron that are learned while it is learning ready, were fixed by most simulations to be $1/R$, which ensures homology in firing rate although these two fractions can differ in real neurons and can vary with time.

3) A Shannon mutual information metric $L = I(\overline{X}, \overline{Y})$ (bits) was derived and evaluated for many illustrative CB neural models. For certain special cases it suggested that more than 1000 bits of information could be stored on single neurons and more than 0.1 bits per synapse.

4) These simulations also demonstrated that the CB false-alarm rate can be less than 1 percent for unlearned random patterns, provided that the

pattern space is sparsely occupied by those patterns that were learned. Moreover, many excitation patterns can be learned by a single neuron, particularly for larger values of the parameters H and R, as limited by the acceptable false alarm rate. This CB model appears to be unique with respect to its combination of learning speed, memory capacity, and neurological plausibility relative to similar hypotheses.

5) Simulations also showed that extensions of the CB neuron model for given values of H and R can learn even more patterns and store more information if they have $C > 1$ independently firing dendrite compartments and $D > 1$ resolvable time slots (that define spike coincidence) located within several milliseconds of its central single neuron excitation pattern, where excitation patterns might excite the neuron at intervals of (say) 25 millisecond or more.

6) Some parameters characterizing the optimum simulated neuron structure depend on the performance metrics being optimized. For example, the synapse-atrophy (SA) simulations suggest in Table 3.4 that larger values of R are best for neurons with larger memories, whereas smaller values of R permit faster response times. Also, higher values of H are more economically efficient when the metabolic cost ratio for neurons to synapses is relatively larger, and vice versa. The importance of these rough results lies principally in their demonstration that such neuron models can suggest potentially testable relationships between neuron properties and their computational function.

4.2 Initial training of multi-layer neural systems

From this point onward the monograph becomes increasingly speculative and should be read in that light. The utility of this speculation, which builds on a plausible spike-based computational foundation, is that it may suggest useful new neural architectures, simulations, and physical experiments, even though real neurons are far more complex.

At birth most cortical connections are random, although the statistical characteristics of neural forms and connectivity are largely predetermined, as is evident in the similarity between neuron types within any species. One classic problem is how the animal's early interaction with its environment might determine these early connections and their strengths, particularly since many neural layers are involved. This question is linked with the more basic question of how cortex thinks.

We hypothesize that the principal initial function of cortex is to memorize the animal's environment and its dynamics, where the environment includes sensory and motor information from the animal itself. The object of memorization is to support superior predictions based on prior observations, and therefore more successful survival and reproduction. The full question of cognizance is postponed.

If the principal initial cortical functions are memorization, recognition, and prediction, then the CB neuron model would seem to suffice as a fundamental computational unit since it can perform those functions alone and in networks. Such a model might be trained sequentially, layer by layer. The connections in the early layers might be determined mostly by genetics, and at the first appropriate higher layer environment-based learning would begin. Since reasonably intelligent behavior is exhibited by social insects having tiny neural circuits coded mostly by genetics, little brain or DNA would seem necessary to survive early infancy in the early absence of full cortical performance. Some small mammals and birds have also packed a surprising amount of innate intelligence, presumably heavily genetic, into very small volumes.

We have assumed that spike-based SS learning occurs only during learning readiness when the firing threshold $G \cdot H$ is effectively temporarily lowered relative to spike amplitudes, and synapses are plastic. Since even bees sense when they are threatened or when they might want to remember the location of food, it is not unreasonable that higher animals could be pre-wired do the same using astrocytes or other cellular intermediaries to lower effective firing thresholds or, equivalently, increase synaptic strengths, and thereby temporarily enable learning within moderately large cortical sectors when such learning is relevant to survival.

Even a general rise in average spiking rate within the immediate neighborhood of a neuron could increase the probability of its firing because there would be more excited inputs, which is equivalent to lowering its threshold $G \cdot H$. Such increases in local firing rates, if sustained, should be evident in increased local metabolic activity visible as small spots in functional MRI images.

One advantage of extended cognons is that they can store much more information per neuron, thus reducing the need for frugality when deciding when local learning readiness (memorization) should start and end.

Under these assumptions of sequential training a multilayer neural network in a newborn might be plastic in only its first layer until that layer had learned the most common neuron excitation features characterizing the infant's environment at that layer. For example, such low level visual system features might include lines, ellipses, or circles of various sizes and orientations that span small local areas. Image-processing researchers often use lapped transform basis functions (Malvar & Staelin, 1989) or similar wavelet functions for compact image representations.

These simpler features or their antecedents could also be genetically prewired, in which case those layers requiring more training would follow the more genetically wired ones. Once any layer's basic features were learned, perhaps by averaging many learning experiences, they could become less plastic or learning ready (i.e., $G \cdot H$ might remain high) while the following neural layer learned excitation patterns formed by the output spikes from the first layer.

A key question for any neuron model is how it would behave in a layered architecture. Fortunately the CB and CE models have hundreds or thousands of inputs and if a single such model can recognize tens or hundreds of unique pattern sets that represent some aspect (feature) of the animal's environment, then each neuron in the next following naïve layer, when it is totally untrained and infantile, could combine such common features from each of hundreds or thousands of similar feature detectors so as to recognize tens or hundreds of super features. By induction, this process can proceed to the top of the stack, many neural levels higher, from a local pixel-oriented sensory domain to a more object-oriented domain at the top.

But why not train all layers, or at least more than one, simultaneously? Consider a deep stack being trained this way, with many layers being learning ready simultaneously. Also suppose there is a

George Washington (GW) neuron near the top of the stack that fires whenever GW is in the visual field anywhere in any position, or is similarly triggered by audio or other cues. When GW is first seen during learning readiness certain random neurons in that high layer would be randomly excited. There is unlikely to be any systematic relation between GW being in the visual field and the excitation of any single object-oriented neuron.

So how can we train each learning-ready layer one at a time successfully? Success requires that the structure of the neural network can accommodate the complexity of those aspects of the environment that promote survival. Animals that can survive if they see flies to eat, avoid predators, and then reproduce successfully need to compute only very simple visual features using very few layers. Humans survive using more complex strategies, but this requires much more sophisticated prediction skills, more features, and more neural layers.

Nonetheless there are limits. For example, we are oblivious to that which we do not see, excellent examples being numerous optical illusions and the well know inability of most viewers to see a gorilla walking through a group of people tossing balls if the viewer is distracted counting the tosses.

That is, our brains have evolved to represent our environment accurately, making compromises when necessary. Another compromise is that different brains probably have different strengths because their various functional regions are generally of different sizes or have different favored connectivity patterns. Not all regions can be large or strongly connected to all other regions. Random responses and inefficient learning are therefore presumably minimized if the initial sequential-layer training occurs in an organized sensory environment representative of that to be experienced later, free from excessive randomness or complexity.

In that fashion an entire stack of layers might be trained sequentially in a very rudimentary way as the animal slowly learned to see. Although the initial learned wiring would almost certainly be non-optimum due to the restricted environments seen by most infants, as the infant ages the synapse distribution and strengths could be slowly optimized through synapse atrophy and addition of new synapses and neurons. Later the possible role and training of feedback will be discussed. This model also suggests the potential importance of the earliest infant environment controlled by parents, particularly if subsequent neural editing is difficult.

Chapter 5

Spike computations, feedback, and cognition

5.1 Training of feedback paths using spikes

It is well known that in many cortical areas there are more feedback synapses conveying information top-down from higher levels than there are synapses conveying information bottom-up from senses such as the visual system (Hawkins & Blakeslee, 2004). Therefore it is important for any learning model to account for top-down feedback synapse training as well. Figure 5.1 illustrates how the CB neuron model and its extensions might accommodate and rapidly train synapses handling such bi-directional flows of information. The afferent synapses for each neuron can be divided into the "A" bottom-up set that accepts spikes from lower sensory layers, and the "B" top-down set that accepts spikes from the outputs of that neural layer and any layer above. Other than this A/B distinction, the only innovation needed to accommodate top-down training is definition of when and where learning readiness is applied.

One simple top-down training option for either an SS or SA neuron N is the following. First, while all B synapses are inactive, synapse set A becomes learning ready and is trained as before, perhaps approaching its maximum number W_A of trainable words. Then set A either raises its firing threshold or lets some unused synapses atrophy, and plasticity moves to those set-B synapses excited by neurons in that same layer. To avoid an undue increase in the firing rate as the set-B synapses are activated either: 1) H is increased slightly, or 2) the less utilized A synapses atrophy, or 3) both might occur. Plasticity for the B set could end intermittently for SS

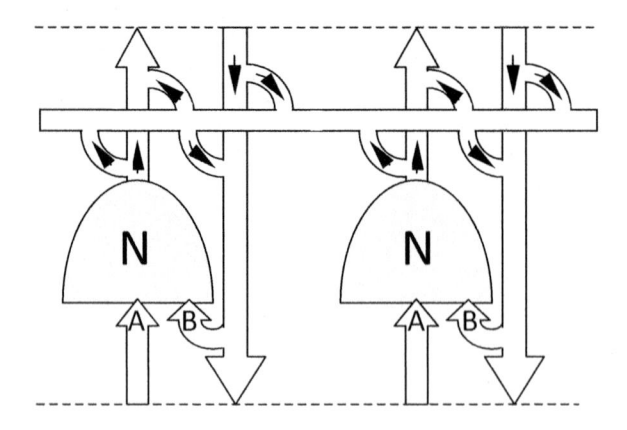

Figure 5.1. Two neural units (N) in a single layer of a dual-flow network having top-down feedback paths. Set-A synapses are feed-forward and Set-B synapses convey feedback.

neurons if learning and recognition alternate, or when the new maximum trainable number of words W_B is reached.

Feedback spikes from the same layer can arrive for some patterns synchronously with the spike produced by synapse set A if neuron N responds later than does its neighbors. Otherwise, that feedback would need to arrive one time-cycle T later to reinforce a repeated presentation of set A. This would require the periods T of these time cycles to be stable within the time resolution for superposition, or perhaps ~1-2 msec if $D > 1$. A likely period T is that associated with gamma waves and attention, or roughly 25 msec (Steinmetz et al., 2000). Any initial feedback within the same spike wave increases the likelihood that a neuron would respond to those patterns to which its neighbors responded, even if it had not learned it using only its own A set. This is also true even if the feedback arrives one or more cycles later because most patterns that are fixed objects of attention would last many cycles (e.g., a mother's face).

Once the A/B set for the first neural layer is trained, then plasticity can pass from the B set of the first neural layer to the A set of the second layer, and then to the second B set, perhaps followed by another round of plasticity for the B set in the first layer. This training cycle (train A, not B;

train B not A) could be repeated for the remaining layers, one layer at a time, as increasingly integrative holistic patterns and concepts form and are memorized at the higher levels. Top-down feedback can originate from one or more levels above the one being trained, particularly if plasticity reappears from time to time at lower levels and if the spike-wave period T is sufficiently stable that such feedback remains synchronous despite being offset one or more periods.

Many variants of this A/B training algorithm are obviously possible. In nature these periods of plasticity, atrophy, and variations in H could overlap in time in a wide variety of ways. For example, it seems likely that alternation between A and B training would be much less necessary in later stages of learning. Alternation could also be avoided or minimized if the B connections formed slowly after training had begun. Also, H could remain roughly constant while one new A or B naïve synapse formed and the least-used synapse atrophied (approximating the SA mode). It is reasonable to assume that nature has evolved a nearly optimum strategy using the full complexity of real neurons, and it is enough for these simple numerical models to demonstrate the plausibility of such strategies.

5.2 Uses for strong spike-based feedback

Such top-down feedback can serve multiple purposes. First, it is clear that if the top-down B feedback corresponds to a preceding spike-wave pattern one or more periods T earlier, then the combined A/B pattern corresponds to a pattern sequence. In the case of visual cortex, such pattern sequences might principally correspond to small features moving in particular directions, changing size, or rotating. For example, one neuron capable of learning 192 visual patterns might instead learn 24 patterns that are moving one spatial step per period T in any of 8 possible directions; such tasks might normally be distributed redundantly over multiple neurons because of the assumed stochastic nature of learning.

Such merged A/B patterns might also correspond to phoneme, musical, motor, or tactile sequences and might subsequently be further merged and lengthened in time via top-down feedback having even longer delays. Sequential storage of memories could provide access to remote memories if a key memory were elicited, followed by sequential access to the forgotten target memory.

Second, if the B set corresponds to approximately the same pattern that is stimulating the A set, then the learned A/B pattern will be more immune to noise than is A alone because H is greater than for A alone and the sets A and B are effectively averaged. Since each B input corresponds to the output of a neuron that may have thousands of other inputs, substantial averaging and noise reduction can occur even if the B set is smaller than the A set.

Noise immunity also increases if the A set is partially predicted by the B set, which is based on earlier inputs. When the excitations for the sets A and B are added and then subjected to a threshold test, an approximately multiplicative term AB is added to the sum, with consequences similar to those of widely used matched filters that improve signal detection in analog receivers. A multiplicative term AB can arise if we approximate the thresholded sum A + B as $(A + B)^2 = A^2 + B^2 + 2AB$, where the average values of A^2 and B^2 are approximately constant and can be subtracted by raising the firing threshold. This effect could significantly enhance the interpretation of speech in noisy environments or of noisy images and night scenes.

Third, to the extent that the B set predicts the A set, the number of A synapses required to lift the excitation sum above H is reduced, and therefore the average number of synapses and bits required to store a given new pattern is reduced, analogous to predictive source encoders used in communications and memory systems. This ability to compress slowly evolving environmental patterns effectively increases the utility of each synapse. Determining quantitatively how the noise reduction, sequence detection, and predictive coding performance of dual-flow neural networks would depend on A, B, and the pattern universe remains an interesting long term problem.

A fourth use may be even more interesting with respect to cognition. An ideal content-addressable or associative memory transmits a stored message after being triggered by a tag or any subset of that message that is sufficiently complex to identify it uniquely. Cortex with feedback can perform that function if the predictive B feedback pattern is more detailed than the sensory pattern that triggers it (Hopfield, 1982; Zheng, Tang, & Zhang, 2010; Hawkins & Blakeslee, 2004). In the CB and CE models presented here the recovered pattern is the collective set of B excitations across multiple neurons, which could also be made available to other neural centers.

Since in the presence of novel inputs the B sets cannot be excited by feedback until the A sets stimulate them, during a recognition task the neuron firing threshold $G \cdot H$ should slowly increase from pattern to pattern at ~25-millisecond intervals as the number of B excitations increases; this also permits multiple neural layers to participate despite their longer round-trip delays. For example, if 12 pattern exposures were required for $G \cdot H$ to fully escalate, then content-addressed patterns would require perhaps 12×25 = 300 msec to emerge, consistent with observations of approximately how long it takes people to identify the contents of an unexpectedly presented new visual scene (Thorpe, Fize, & Marlot, 1996).

In some cases a single stimulating sub-pattern might potentially correspond to two different full patterns, in which case only one can "win." That is, the feedback can readily confirm only one or the other interpretation at one time. If the winning full pattern employs synapses that slowly exhaust their biochemical resources, then the alternate pattern may suddenly win instead, and this alternation could continue for multiple cycles, consistent with multistable perception and the well-known three-dimensional Necker cube illusion. It would interesting to know if the frequency of oscillation in illusions similar to the Necker cube is correlated with the replacement rates of exhaustible biochemical resources. For example, are oscillations faster in older or other subjects who tire sooner when thinking?

5.3 Cognition with spikes

The seat and nature of cognition have been historically elusive and controversial, and this monograph can do little more than to speculate how a spike-based learning and recognition system might support or refine hypotheses discussed by others (Hawkins & Blakeslee, 2004; Koch, 2004).

Consider, for example, how we might be able to perceive a perfectly straight line using only model neurons that spike when perhaps ten input spikes arrive at the same time. Suppose that at lower levels of the visual system we have neurons Q1 that spike when pixels (picture elements) in their small local region are excited. Suppose a neuron Q2 in the next layer then learns to spike when four or five such Q1 well-separated neurons lying in approximately the same straight line are excited. Because the sensitivity regions for each Q1 are blurry circles, each Q2 responds to independent jagged straight lines. However, if multiple Q2's then stimulate a Q3 neuron in the following layer, that Q3 neuron will respond to a less jagged average of these Q2 jagged straight lines.

Although additional neural layers and averaging can result in responses that are increasingly indicative of perfectly straight lines, fewer layers would be required if the upper perception is of a perfectly straight line which is approximated by spike patterns propagating downward toward the sensory layers. If the upward and downward pattern streams agree then the perceived straight line is validated.

If the sensed straight line moves, then validation would fail and the error signals fed upward would cause the perceived line to move correspondingly. Whether this is how straight lines are in fact perceived would be difficult to determine, and many coding schemes are possible and may even be used in parallel. Another scheme involves averaging local pixel positions first rather than averaging jagged lines. The point is that spike patterns can plausibly support perception of straight lines or any other visual, auditory, olfactory, tactile, emotional, or other sensation.

We next ask what it means to perceive something. For example, one can see, feel, taste, hold, and smell an apple all at the same time one is sensing the associated kitchen, companions, mood, weather, motor system state, etc. These are sensed jointly, not in isolation, although we may choose to focus on taste or companions alone. Thus the meaning of "apple" can extend beyond the object itself. These associated memories in different cortical regions presumably help trigger each other through the inter-regional communications connections provided by white matter so as to produce an integrated perception.

But what is it that we sense? Is it the processed upward-moving signals from our various internal and external sensory systems, the downward-moving signals, or something else? Since the visual signals propagating downward sometimes out-number those propagating upward by perhaps ten to one, it is reasonable to assume that the representational accuracy propagating downward toward the senses is of better quality, and that the upward signals merely ensure that the internal cognitive view of the world is consistent. For example, the optical signals arriving at the retina are distorted on the sidewalls of the retina, exhibit diffraction fringes, and illuminate blind spots, but nonetheless do not usually degrade the internal visual view of the world. Furthermore, our three-dimensional "hyper-vision" view of the world has no counterpart in the raw senses and clearly was constructed at the higher neural levels.

We could take the liberty of calling our conscious view of the world a hallucination because it is a fabricated representation that differs from our sensed signals in important ways, but fortunately it is often better than that imperfectly sensed reality. Relative to our imperfect senses it is a synthesized "super-reality." Our resulting perception of the world and our consciousness are therefore constructed principally in cortex in association with other brain elements and are healthy so long as they agree well with the external world.

Thus, healthy cortex must continually compare its upward and downward flowing information and detect inconsistencies at each level that can be fed upward as an error pattern permitting perceptual corrections; for example, a viewed object may have moved slightly. Persistent mismatches between internal and external reality in one or more senses are generally diagnosed as hallucinations indicative of schizophrenia.

Figure 5.2 illustrates how the apparently uni-directional neural network of Figure 5.1 is topologically equivalent to a symmetric network for which the upward and downward information flows can be the same if enough axons and/or dendrites extend both upward and downward. Note that even though all neurons point upward, the numbers of pure "up" and "down" paths can be equal, as suggested by the two dashed flow lines. In nature many neurons are effectively fully inverted, with more axons

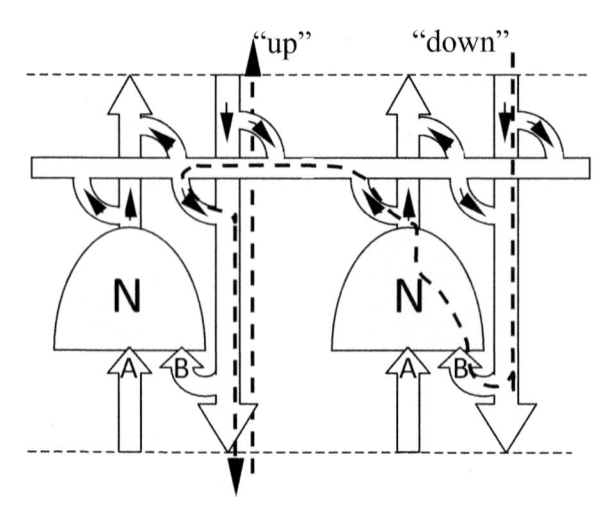

Figure 5.2. Symmetric dual-flow network having equal numbers of "up" and "down" paths, indicated by dashed lines, and possibly equal numbers of A (feed-forward) and B (feedback) synapses per neuron.

emerging below than above, and this geometry is simpler than the one suggested in the figure.

For true symmetry the numbers of A and B synapses are equal, and the result is a symmetric "dual-flow" neural network. Any degree of asymmetry can be accommodated by changing the synapse ratio of A to B. One point of this observation is that the CB spike-processing learning and recall models discussed above in the context feedback networks apply equally well when many neurons face backwards because the two situations are topologically equivalent.

Figure 5.3 suggests schematically how a dual-flow cortex might be stabilized so both flows are "locked" together. Locking implies that the "up" information for each pattern (say 25-ms separations) is accurately predicted by the "down" information so that relatively few error bits (represented by spikes, one per pattern per neuron detecting an error) suffice to correct the subsequent prediction. Almost certainly such locking must occur between every important pair of neural levels because each spike and correction conveys no more than one bit per pattern comparison

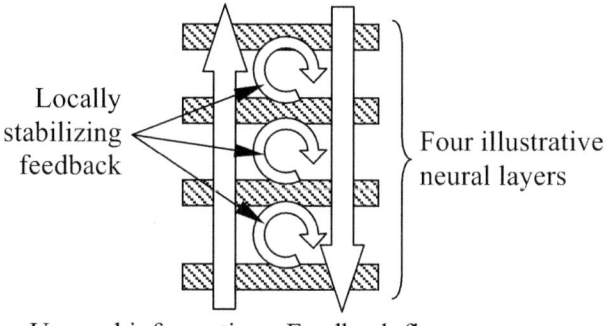

Figure 5.3. Schematic of local feedback stabilization in a multi-level neural network.

per neuron (for the best case, half of all pattern changes cause a given neuron to spike).

One interesting consequence of feedback and dual-flow locking is that if inter-pattern time separations (T's) differ sufficiently, then further distinctions between patterns and pattern types could be achieved within single neurons. Adding such frequency-domain multiplexing to population-delay coding could be particularly useful for boosting the communications and addressing capabilities of white matter.

Without closed-loop control of the internal cognition system the brain is forced to synthesize an internal reality that can range from amusing to highly dangerous. For example, drugs and other extreme conditions can disrupt control and produce hallucinations. But how do spike-based cognon models support this view of cognition? We have shown that even the simple CB neuron model can learn to recognize patterns, and have discussed how neurons approximately arranged in layers could plausibly do the same over large fields of visual or other data at any of many hierarchical cortical levels.

The next question is how spike processing might compare two patterns and provide useful information about their differences that can be fed upward in order to correct perception at higher neural levels. Although how this occurs is unclear, one possibility is that subtraction is effectively achieved simply because the forward and backward A and B patterns superimpose to meet the firing threshold only if they agree. If they don't agree and therefore fail to meet the firing threshold, then that neuron won't fire, which could inform the higher levels of a defect without specifying what it is beyond the identity of that particular neuron with its unique AB ensemble of connections.

Since multiple closely neighboring neurons probably perform similar computations for the same local image, and their pattern sensitivities are different, then it is plausible that the ensemble of "difference" signals from a full set of neighbors could collectively provide the necessary corrective information. This information could be interpreted based on which neurons perceived an error and therefore failed to fire for that period T. The high-level neurons would then change state to eliminate the errors and update the perception. Local motion compensation alone should correct most errors.

The bit rate per neuron for corrective information sent upward can be crudely estimated by noting that addition of A and B excitations to meet a threshold would produce a spike most of the time if reality remained constant and there were no errors. When a particular correction is needed the spike might not appear, which corresponds to less than one bit if $D = 1$, and very slightly more otherwise because the time of appearance might be within any one of D possible time slots. Since many neighboring neurons are probably performing very similar comparisons, the error detection process can be both robust and more information rich than if a single neuron carried the full error-detection burden.

Under this model if an object remained unchanged for too long, all neurons detecting no error would spike at period T and thus quickly exhaust certain neurotransmitter resources in the active neurons. One result after resource exhaustion could be failure to spike, suggesting continual errors over any affected object and causing the brain to infer visual failure and "paper over" that object with the locally surrounding visual field, much as it does with other blind spots. Thus staring at objects should cause them to fade under both this model and others. Since saccades guarantee rapid scene changes, they could reduce this problem posed by viewed stationary objects.

If there is a second interpretation of the same visual field involving different neurons then, if the primary neurons exhaust their resources, that alternate interpretation might temporarily take precedence, as suggested earlier for the Necker cube illusion. Note that this interpretation would not produce the Necker cube illusion if the feedback comparison involved B synapses that were inhibitory rather than excitatory because in that case agreement between up and down signals produces no spikes, and would not do so if the sum were further impaired by neurotransmitter exhaustion.

Thus, cognition may best be understood as the internal fantasy world of the mind that integrates all internal and external sensory data to model, predict, and control mind and body. This modeling ability can also partially extend to the minds and bodies of others. Evidence suggests, for example, that some people can accurately mimic in their minds the motor control commands that correspond to those utilized by others they watch, such as sports heroes or ballerinas, and thus learn the same moves by intellectual imitation.

The same neural mimicry seems to be true for the emotions of people highly sensitive to others, or for those who truly feel the pain of others. These traits vary widely from person to person, however. Each person therefore presumably experiences cognition in slightly different ways, depending on which brain sectors are most talented and developed. For example, verbal and spatial skills vary widely from person to person, as do memory, analytical skills, coordination, emotional control, etc. "Super-vision" may also differ but cannot be readily measured. The degree to which these differences are genetic, developmental, or educational is not well known, but it is clear that all three can sometimes play dominant roles, particularly when establishing upper bounds on performance.

5.4 Inter-regional training and communication via white matter

The nature of synapse training is different during "boot-up" in newborns before there is apt cortical wiring and strengthening of synapses, and later during normal operation after rudimentary feature definitions have been established by such wiring and synapse training at each level of a neural network. Both these boot-up and operational training issues also arise when neural links are established in white matter in order to communicate between different cortical regions. Such white matter learning and signaling mechanisms are still very poorly understood.

We conjecture that once each sensory, motor, and conceptual region has locally established its initial synaptic and feature structure at its middle and higher levels, it can begin to emulate an independent sensory area that can boot-up and train neurons in white matter to serve as useful links to other cortical regions. It could also simultaneously train any feedback neurons in such links and perhaps gain one or more of their advantages (noise reduction, sequence perception, compression, and associative memory capabilities). Passage of white-matter neurons through the thalamus also offers an opportunity for spike and pattern synchronization since it is known to have a timing function of unclear nature.

The plausibility of this white-matter communications hypothesis rests largely on that of the similar training protocols and operations proposed for multi-layer neural networks employing feedback in Section 5.1. In an abstract sense such multi-layer spiking networks with significant feedback have no "top" or "bottom," just two ends providing stochastically complex but sparse behavior that maps well end-to-end across multiple neural layers. That is, all environmentally meaningful and distinct events might plausibly map across the neural network of interest, e.g., through white matter plus any interface logic, to their corresponding interpretations, and vice versa.

For example, several high-level auditory features in combination might trigger one or a few visual responses, while several combined high-level visual features or objects might trigger one or a few auditory responses in a dual-direction hierarchy. If such signals "ping-pong" end to end a few times they would tend to arrive at one preferred solution, much as broadband oscillators tend to settle near the single frequency that has the largest round-trip gain. This differs from a unidirectional hierarchy where, for example, information might typically progress from pixels toward objects, or vice versa, but not both simultaneously.

While training inter-regional white-matter links there presumably would be considerable interference due to ongoing cognitive processes unless the animal were fully passivated or asleep. If asleep then the firing threshold could more safely be lowered to allow synapse-strength (SS) cognons to learn with less "attention noise". Equivalent changes in neurotransmitters could also boost spike amplitudes with the same increase in the probability of learning.

But if inter-regional learning occurs during sleep it would help to know what drives it, such as replayed memories. Therefore it would be interesting to see if certain sleep regimes are associated with replayed memories, and whether some memories are synchronized between sensory and other modalities, such as memories involving both viewed seagulls and the sounds of their cries, or memories that link the motor cortex with spatial memory in the hippocampus. This inter-regional (white-matter) training hypothesis appears to be consistent with the widespread belief that sleep helps consolidate recent memories (Stickgold, 2005), and may correspond to one of the sequential stages of sleep. If natural periodicities could be associated with particular interregional pathways, perhaps those periods could reveal the sleep stage involved.

Based on the polynomial approximation at the bottom of Table 3.5 for the communications capability (bits/second/neuron) of a single homologous SA model neuron optimized for maximum L, there seems to be little advantage to using $D > 1$ (patterns that use more than one intra-pattern ~1-millisecond time slot) for white-matter communications. However, it should be easy to optimize neural learning for communications capacity (bits/second/neuron) instead of L (bits/neuron), thus revealing whether there are any advantages to having $D > 1$ in that more plausible case; but this has not yet been done.

If $D = 1$ because there are no computational advantages to $D > 1$ for the CB model, then it should be easier to interpret observed white-matter communications, assuming enough neurons in any bundle could be monitored (a major experimental challenge). In fact, the homologous SA model neurons optimized for L seem to communicate a relatively constant number of bits/neuron/second, and to store a relatively constant number of bits/synapse, where the maximum packing density of both neurons and synapses is reasonably constant for biological reasons. Brain volume may therefore primarily limit both the total bits/brain and total bits/second/brain for SA L-optimized model neurons, where these two metrics may depend relatively little on parameters like C, D, and S_o. Readers who skipped chapters 2 and 3 might best jump to Chapter 6.

One potential exception may be a dependence upon brain simplicity. For example, Table 3.5 suggests on its second and last lines, respectively, that the bits/synapse and bits/neuron/second for optimized neurons vary inversely with R and H, whereas the fourth line suggests that the number of mature synapses S_m, and hence neuron size, increases with R and H. Tables 2.3 and 2.4 yield a similar conclusion: simpler neurons appropriate for insects and small animals can be more efficient per synapse and per bit, but are nonetheless disfavored relative to more powerful brains when the cognitive challenges are greater.

5.5 Approaches to analyzing neural networks with rich feedback

The most tractable approach for adapting this extended spike-based CE neuron learning model to the rich feedback case is probably to continue limiting the initial studies to the additive processes discussed in Section 5.2 that can arguably detect pattern sequences, improve signal-to-noise ratios, offer advantages of source coding, and enable content-addressable or associative memory. All these benefits seem addressable using single-neuron simulations and, with some creativity, may be partially addressed analytically.

Although neural models with some inhibitory synapses may more readily approximate direct subtraction, the data rate for the error information sent upward per A+B comparison neuron, even using inhibition, could not easily exceed roughly one bit (based on one spike) per pattern change (each change represents a difference between expectation and reality). Given the increased complexity of mixing excitation and inhibition synapses, and the expected limited increases in pattern-correction information available per neuron, inhibition studies might usefully be postponed until the limits of simple additive processes are better understood.

Once single-neuron training and performance are understood, several individually optimized neuron models might be arranged in two layers that could be simulated as before, with a training period followed by recall tests that measure recognition performance for learned and novel excitation patterns applied to the first neural layer.

Application of these initial results to white matter communications with rich feedback might begin with a symmetric network with equal numbers of A and B synapses on each neuron so there is no "top" end.

Chapter 6

Waking visual anomalies, hallucinations, and cognons

6.1   Observations and interpretations of waking visual anomalies

Due to their brevity (less than a few seconds) and character, waking visual anomalies (WVA) appear to be a new phenomenon reported here for the first time, although some might consider them a subset of hypnopompic anomalies (anomalies experienced upon waking), which are often experienced minutes to hours after subjects awake. In any event WVA appear to be inadequately documented. WVA may also be related, for example, to the brief hypnagogic illusions (anomalies experienced while first falling asleep) reported by subjects subsequent to playing the computer game Tetris (Stickgold *et al.*, 2000).

WVA were observed on multiple occasions by the lead author (DHS) and are detailed here. One reason WVA anomalies are seemingly unknown is that they are very infrequent and typically last less than a few seconds upon waking. Moreover, they can occupy only a portion of the visual field and always disappear instantly when one opens one's eyes to the light. For these reasons they are more difficult to study than the more common longer lasting hypnagogic and hypnopompic illusions. DHS does not recall ever having either post-sleep hypnopompic or pre-sleep hypnagogic experiences.

We hypothesize that WVA occur when some small part of the cortex awakes unevenly, resulting in local or foveal failure to lock together the upward and downward flowing information. These very brief failures lead to local perceptual errors manifest as WVA. They presumably last until the control loop system suggested in Figure 5.3 locks the upward and downward information flows together.

When they are not locked, the downward flow is apparently perceived as it exists near the neural layer where locking failed, thus possibly providing clues to the processing that may occur in that neural layer of the human visual system. As explained later these clues suggest how some neurons or layers might code images using spatial basis functions and time-domain multiplexing, and that the human brain may have the ability to record and replay "movies," sometimes in reverse at high speed.

Because of the potential implications of these observations, it is important to understand why they have not been widely reported before. First, they are extremely rare; most of the individual WVA observations reported here were separated by months to decades, representing a lifetime average of roughly one second of data per year, concentrated after age 65. Second, a WVA immediately vanishes when the two-way signal flow locks together, so the observer has to be quick (< 1 second) to sense that the phenomenon is present and then make a conscious effort to remember and report what was seen. This seems unlikely unless the observer deduces its neurological and cognitive implications or is a study participant. Third, most people experiencing such a rare and brief event would no doubt open their eyes and forget about it. Finally, based on one subject, WVA occurs primarily in infants or in the elderly, not unlike the hypnopompic state.

The subject, DHS, is an exception because sometime before age three he became sensitized to WVA when he awoke from a nap facing a strange carpet over the edge of a bed. His field of view was initially filled with swirling colored paisley patterns that slowed within 2-3 seconds and became the patterns on a previously unnoticed oriental rug. This was his first retained memory because it was so interesting, and it sensitized him to recurrences, all of which then occurred after age 55. By then he had become sufficiently immersed in image processing and coding issues that, despite their brevity, these WVA events were technically informative. We now conjecture that the swirling was the young brain's attempt to reconcile the strange new pattern with prior memories using only weak corrective signals that required a couple of seconds to lock together the upward and downward flows of information.

The next remembered individual WVA occurrences were spaced at intervals of several years. At first a transient set of dark almond shapes would typically flash randomly and independently in time, position, and orientation, where perhaps 10-20 might fit across an approximately foveal field of view and only 10 shapes might be visible at a time (corresponding perhaps to $R \cong 30$), where each "frame" lasted less than 0.2 seconds and probably was the result of a sliding time window integrating ovals that flashed much faster. A rough representation of such an instantaneous image appears in Figure 6.1(a); it was observed for less than a few seconds on perhaps three or four occasions.

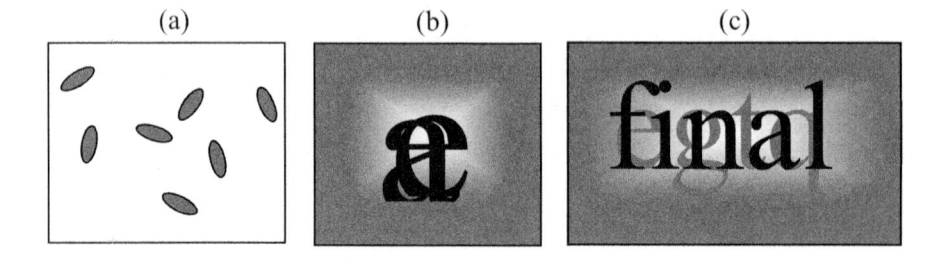

Figure 6.1. Approximate renditions of perceived transient waking anomalies that typically lasted 1-3 seconds and changed at rates roughly between 12 and 30 Hz; the overlapped instantaneous images suggest the higher rates.

These natural experiments suggest that some single level in the feedback system might be temporarily unsynchronized so as to reveal at least one of the dominant features utilized at that level. In this view such ovals might correspond roughly to some subset of wavelet-like basis functions created by a neuron or neural column that is asynchronously flashing inappropriately, and this malfunction is being perceived correctly. That is, if the upward flow is asynchronous or random at some neural level then the perceived features will not be stable but will change randomly, perhaps at 30-millisecond intervals. These features would presumably be restricted to those features characterized at that level at that time. The fact that WVA disappear instantly when the eyes see a bright scene suggests that WVA end when perceptions lock to a stronger image, ignoring the weak malfunctioning signals.

Another brief WVA (4 seconds, age 72) involved a pure motion field of densely spaced tiny differently colored single-pixel-sized dots approximately filling the foveal field and moving in a swirling pattern. The dots were spaced several dot diameters apart. At one location the motion's radius of curvature was only a few such pixels, and perhaps even one or two. The dot velocities were such that a dot might cross the field in 4-8 seconds. Since a key metric of motion fields is their spatial resolution and this image resolution appeared to be on the order of a few pixels or less, the motion field alone conveyed substantial information, again illustrating the incredible image-generating power of the mind. Because of the large scale organization of this WVA, it probably was created at a higher level and arose because of a lack of sensory input.

A different set of WVA's began in 2007 (age 68) and immediately led to the initial analyses and simulations that underlie this monograph. The initial image lay in the lower left quadrant of the visual field and consisted of just one tiny white circle containing partial segments of what appeared to be many letters of the alphabet, for example, perhaps a piece of an "e" or a "g" in black ink. Figure 6.1(b) suggests the nature of this dynamic image, the diameter of which might have been about one-twentieth that of the foveal field. The figure is misleading in that only about half a letter was actually observable within the white circle. It was presented for less than three seconds at more than 10 frames per second and therefore was only barely discerned.

Because of the image's small size and limited total number of pixels, say 200, it was conjectured that perhaps only one neuron or one column of neurons might be asynchronously firing rapidly, randomly transmitting members of its library of features that subsequent neurons might normally be able to interpret if they were properly synchronized. It is reasonable to assume that the upper neural levels correctly reported this asynchronous firing since the individual image flashes make sense as members of a useful library of options for particular tasks.

These observations do not clearly distinguish between two types of feature coding: population vs. time-multiplexed coding. The codes described in Chapter 2 are population codes for which the subset of excited input neurons conveys the information. Time-multiplexed codes can convey information using the ~2-millisecond time slot at which the output soma fires, which could be one of several available within the inter-pattern period of perhaps 30 milliseconds. Each time slot would correspond to a different feature. Population coding could produce random patterns if the neurons were firing randomly, perhaps due to low firing thresholds, and time-multiplexed codes could produce random patterns for the same reason or because the timing of the two information flows became unsynchronized at that neural level.

Initially we interpreted each mistimed spike as a different pre-learned image associated with its own learned time slot within a presumed gamma-wave or other periodic cycle. The initial concept in 2007 was therefore that the exact timing of a neuron's output spike might indicate the recognized feature, or letter of the alphabet in this case, using time-division multiplexing like that used in some communications systems.

This speculative conjecture concerning time-multiplexed pattern recognition within single neurons led to development of a $D > 1$ neural model over the next few years, which then led to the current family of extended cognon neural models. A couple of years then passed before the second time-multiplexing WVA was observed and interesting suggestions of photographic recall started to appear.

These suggestions of photographic recall began with a WVA that again occupied a small percentage of the foveal field and was again off center to the lower left. It had a light beige oval or hotdog-shaped background that encircled perhaps several letters of the alphabet, where the entire set of letters was again being replaced at the same 10-20 Hz rate (full letters, not fragments). Figure 6.1(c) approximates this image at one instant, as perceived with some time overlap.

This general illusion recurred perhaps three times at intervals of months to a year with the number of letters increasing slightly each time. On the last occasion, the letters "Jenn" may have been discerned briefly, these being the first four letters of the name of a recently frequent email correspondent, as recent as the previous day. This very tenuous evidence suggested these word fragments might conceivably represent very recent photographic memories of a viewed LCD computer screen, a highly speculative hypothesis that was partially reinforced shortly by other observations. It is probably relevant that DHS spent much time viewing black letters on a white LCD display that flickers at a high rate; the flicker may be relevant because WVA often involve highly dynamic LCD images, and the flicker may resonate with certain natural EEG frequencies.

Much later (age 73) another type of WVA apparently probed a third neural level where the faint image of text was nearly foveal and appeared to be convolved with a Laplacian that produced ringing around the edges of the letters while retaining zero-mean intensity across the text. The half-power width of the Laplacian might have been approximately one-fifth the widths of the letters. This WVA appeared twice, once when stationary (nearly invisible) and once when moving at normal non-reversed velocities.

Another type of WVA suggesting photographic memory lasted roughly up to three to five seconds. These WVA events occurred perhaps 6-8 times at intervals of months and usually after a nap or the next morning following DHS's generation, editing, and display of text on a 24-inch flat panel computer display. Such editing often ended by scrolling entire lengthy manuscripts, start to finish, looking for obvious format problems at perhaps one or two pages per second; the font was dark gray on a white background. In this case the scrolled text often moved up the screen at that speed. In marked contrast, the WVA often consisted of full-page-width text with paragraph indentations and separations moving downward several times faster in the opposite direction. This was a time-reversed accelerated replay of what appeared to be scrolling text. The font seemed too small or blurred to read, even if it had moved more slowly, whereas the original font was legible when static.

Two other related WVA's occurred a few weeks later, this time with nearly static fields of text lasting about 4-6 seconds. The first was of a large nearly stationary full-page-width textual image of nearly legible gray text on a white background that was missing narrow meandering streaks that randomly ran through it diagonally, leaving roughly 6-10 large islands of full text several words wide.

The second and most surprising event was again a full-width stretch of similarly stationary complete text, approximately foveal, that was dynamically being erased from the end at a pace that exceeded normal typing speeds by a factor of at least five. The timing of the erasures was consistent with irregular typing of phrases. Thus it was apparently another example of an accelerated time-reversed foveal memory with full-page content. The text probably would have been barely legible had the dynamics not been so distracting.

Because of the potential significance of human accelerated or time-reversed recall processes, it is important to have confirming evidence. One independent observation supporting the hypothesis that humans may experience time-reversed or accelerated visual memory replay was reported for one subject who visualized sequential erasure of rows of Tetris blocks during a hypnogogic memory that lasted several seconds and followed hours of playing Tetris on the computer screen; several other subjects visualized instead falling Tetris blocks that built up layers as they accumulated (Stickgold *et al.*, 2000).

Tetris is a computer game that requires the player to manipulate falling blocks so as to build up layers of them at the bottom of the screen in the shortest possible time. Since it takes at least many seconds to a minute to build a Tetris layer, erasure of two or more layers within a few seconds implies time acceleration. In all Tetris and DHS observations no surround was visualized, just dynamic blocks, text, or ellipses.

Similar evidence of accelerated replay of visual features may also reside in hypnogogic events lasting a few seconds, such as the privately reported illusions of windmills and propellers rotating sufficiently fast to form a partial blur with a clear direction of motion. These illusions perhaps correspond to time-multiplexed coding of bar-angle outputs from known neural complexes that define rotational angles of bars and that are perhaps located in the preceding neural level.

These time-reversed and time-accelerated events are so singular and have such import that it is useful to rule out alternative explanations, such as meaningless hallucinations. As noted earlier, WVA's occur only at waking, last less than a few seconds while the subject is fully conscious and aware of reality, and usually consist of images moving or changing at abnormally high rates. In contrast, hallucinations usually resemble reality or reasonable distortions of it, and tend not to be time-compressed, quite unlike high speed "untyping" or erasure of layers of Tetris blocks.

The high speed reverse-time presentation of these waking visual anomalies (WVA) is most interesting in view of numerous observations of the dreaming patterns of rats that sometimes trace their steps in a maze in reverse order, from cheese to entrance. These dreams, sensed by arrays of electrical probes in the rat's hippocampus, occur at speeds that are several times faster than in life, although time is not always reversed and the time scales are not always compressed (Davidson, Kloosterman, & Wilson; 2009).

Two-dimensional video recordings played back in reverse at high speed, even in black and white, are extremely difficult to explain unless time is mapped to space, probably in the hippocampus. For example, if video frames were arranged in a linear spatial sequence, first to last, then a frame trigger that moves forward or backward through space/time at a rate determined by a variable clock might explain such variability. But how such a memory array would be structured, trained, and triggered for replay is unclear.

These WVA pose another problem. If they are time-multiplexed they suggest that there are more time slots, within which one feature is recognized, in each inter-pattern period than seem plausible in view of the discussion in Section 3.3 relative to gamma waves (period of ~30 milliseconds). For example, in a 30-millisecond period there are fewer than $30/2 = 15$ 2-millisecond time slots available. However, if WVA memories are associated with inter-regional or other communications operating in the 1-5 Hz region, they might accommodate over 100 time slots rather than fewer than 15. In this case the period with which the WVA cycling features reappeared could be 0.2–1 second; unfortunately this period was not discernable because the features cycled too fast.

Since most mammals exhibit similar brain function, perhaps the observed accelerated and time-reversed phenomena are shared too. However, such time-reversed recall across species seems highly unlikely unless it reflects fundamental computational functions, such as the linking of inter-regional memories or the reinforcement or erasure of memory sequences. WVA-like phenomena appear to offer the only easy window into such mechanisms in humans because WVA reveal what the sleeping brain was thinking in the absence of the noise of consciousness. However, the anomaly is visible only for a maximum of a few seconds until a slow-to-awake sensory system takes over and ends it. Hypnagogic memories sometimes provide similar insights and typically last longer (Stickgold *et al.*, 2000).

Since viewing a computer screen before sleeping produced such WVA on multiple occasions, it may be possible for others to confirm these observations. The best subjects are probably older, perhaps over 65, and therefore presumably more susceptible to transient waking anomalies that rely on slow-to-awake neural sub-networks. It is interesting to note that the duration, field of view, and frequency of the WVA increased slowly with the subject's age, and then more rapidly as health began to decline after age 70.

These WVA, taken together, arguably provide useful clues about the human visual system and its memory and processing mechanisms at various neural levels. These clues might help guide theoretical and simulation-based approaches to understanding cortical computations based on spike processing. Until such experiments can be systematized and repeated their utility will be restricted to suggesting new research directions. Perhaps exposing subjects to similar images at different flicker rates during the day may stimulate such WVA, but the multiyear intervals between some occurrences suggest that any strategy may be difficult, particularly in view of the typical 1-3 second durations of WVA and the need for attentive observers.

6.2 Experiments in initiating and terminating hallucinations

The following observations by DHS and others are different in kind from those of WVA. Most of these phenomena are neither brief nor associated with waking. They are included here because they tend to reinforce the feedback model of Figure 5.3, which suggests how local sensory spike-based patterns could excite increasingly global spike-based concepts at successively higher neural levels, and vice versa. They also suggest how disruptions in the consistency or "lock" between these two information flows would force the upper levels to imagine reality and hallucinate, and how strengthening the sensory stream can restore lock and abruptly end weak visual, auditory, and olfactory hallucinations.

The first set of illusions and hallucinations were induced by strong pain-killers. These illusions were weak and occurred during full consciousness while DHS drifted into and out of sleep at perhaps 5-10 minute intervals during the night following surgery. That night offered many opportunities to perform experiments with illusions, where each illusion lasted a minute or two. Alternatively each illusion was easily ended at will by fully opening the eyes in the partially darkened room to view a clock on the opposite wall. The clock was sufficiently distinct to lock perception to reality and immediately terminate the visual effect. DHS had never been exposed to hallucinogens prior to this, and had never experienced any hallucinations

At first it was difficult to elicit these illusions because they usually evolved over a minute or so and viewing the clock promptly ended them; keeping the eyes nearly closed soon solved that problem. Once ended by opening the eyes, no illusion reappeared without a similar rebuilding delay of perhaps half a minute or more, and usually only after a new awakening. These illusions initially evolved slowly from blackness into a uniform flat fabric of similar darkness except that the warp and woof slowly became clearer. As the hours passed more elaborate illusions were teased into being, each evolving slightly faster but still lasting less than a minute or two. First, the fabric typically tended to evolve into more elaborate but generally similar static images.

Perhaps the most illuminating was wall-to-wall randomly shaped and positioned round and oblong grey and brown pebbles, perhaps 20 in each direction over an approximate foveal field. These illusions were roughly circular and not "wide screen." Next a realistic flowing water stream slowly took form above the pebbles, implying that the illusion had properly superimposed a transparent dynamic multi-direction motion field in front of a static one. Finally the illusion slowly added solar highlights on the water surface that realistically moved as the water flowed, thereby adding a third distinct motion field superimposed on the other two. And this was done with spikes.

One might suppose that such a complex three-motion-field image could only be synthesized by viewing nature and locking to it, yet this was synthesized totally internally in real time, a difficult real-time image generation challenge even for powerful computers. DHS had seen such illuminated streams in nature so the scene was not pure fabrication. These first observations of weak-hallucination initiation and termination later led to another series of informal experiments and anecdotes discussed in Section 6.3.

These experiments in the initiation and control of illusions or partial hallucinations motivated additional natural experiments of opportunity that are more anecdotal than formal, but nonetheless may be informative. The first set involved auditory hallucinations suffered by several strangers who phoned DHS with concerns that someone was talking or listening to them or to someone they cared for, and possibly even controlling them using radio waves. Claimed curiosity about radio-wave behavior was usually the stated purpose of the call. In most cases respectful discussions of the symptoms suggested that the subject was probably experiencing hallucinations and was likely to be schizophrenic. When discussed later with psychiatrists this diagnosis was usually found plausible.

One call about the radio-wave hypothesis was from a woman in her 40's who lived with her mother and who had been mostly unemployed since childhood because she often heard voices. Since she did not always hear them, the feedback loops appeared to be marginally functional. This observation led to the hypothesis that if she increased the intensity of the ambient auditory input, the resulting increased error signal in the feedback control system might enable her consciousness to lock to it so that the audio hallucination would disappear. In partial confirmation she then volunteered that her problem was most prevalent when the room was quiet and that when she listened to music the problem was not there, although she had never connected these two facts.

DHS then suggested that any time voices bothered her she might listen to a music or radio source using unobtrusive ear buds or the equivalent. She seemed delighted because her prior experience had taught her that the music trick was both simple and effective. In fact, student psychiatrists are sometimes taught that music can control mild auditory hallucinations.

About two years after this story had been shared with a psychiatrist at a party, he cited the case of a young patient in his twenties whom he had consequently advised to buy headphones and a music source. This patient, previously unemployed for a long period, then soon found employment as a cook. It therefore seems plausible that many cases of mild auditory hallucinations could be helped by unobtrusive audio input.

It is not obvious that strengthening external stimuli would restore healthy locking of consciousness to reality. For example, if $A < B$ and if the error signal $|A - B|$ is inadequate to lock the loop (where A and B refer to the synapse sets illustrated in Figure 5.1), then it would seem that $|2A - B|$ might be even more inadequate. However if the control system were alternatively designed to ignore error signals when either A or B is too weak and therefore noisy because there are too few spikes, then increasing A to 2A could indeed close an open control loop.

That nature would disable noisy feedback circuits makes sense, particularly if other sensory signals can stabilize the perception of reality, just as blind people can "see" using auditory and other inputs. Traumatic or even unpleasant thoughts and events might also be tolerated better by temporarily breaking such loops and substituting helpful hallucinations or illusions. Such illusions could even be conceptual, where an unpleasant thought, such as losing an unaffordable bet, could be replaced by the temporary non-adaptive thought of winning the next bigger bet. Similarly, the health consequences of a midnight trip to the refrigerator, or those of unethical behavior, could be ignored by the stress-induced temporary unlocking of white matter links between areas of the brain involving judgment and desires.

Another potential application of strengthened stimuli is to post-traumatic stress disorder (PTSD) patients who suffer from occasional mild flashbacks. The hope is that such hallucinations might be terminated by strong orthogonal signals, such as newscasts from an exciting football game, that introduce a different reality of sufficient sensory and emotional strength for the patient that the new "reality" could lock perception to itself and thereby terminate the flashback. Only careful experiments could determine the practical utility of this hypothesis. If the hypothesis is valid, then perhaps sensitive body-mounted stress and function sensors could introduce such distracting and reality-restoring sounds automatically when needed, but much testing would be needed.

Hallucinations can also be olfactory. A unique and brief experience of DHS with olfactory hallucinations was probably enabled by an imperfect air flight under some stress at age 72. It was then probably triggered by residual smoke in the hotel room because at first that was the only place the smell was evident and long lasting. The same smell then appeared the next day outdoors and typically lasted for many seconds or more after an outer sweater, worn earlier in the hotel room, was brushed. Over a period of a week or so the false smell became more common and less dependent on the sweater, which led to the hypothesis it might be an olfactory hallucination.

This olfactory hallucination typically lasted from a few seconds up to a minute at most. Over the following few weeks it occurred perhaps an average of once per day in odor-free environments for typical durations that shortened gradually to the 1-2 second duration of a single soft inhalation. It could be terminated by smelling something else, although later its natural duration became so short that this experiment could no longer be performed.

The most effective trigger for this olfactory hallucination seemed to be the combination of a normal brief soft inhalation plus some uncertainty or self-doubt, although that would not explain its rarity. The triggering smell also slowly drifted slightly toward more acidity. A seemingly effective test of whether the smell was a hallucination was to inhale more strongly a few seconds afterward, and on those occasions no such smell was noted. That is, the trigger was highly specific and apparently included the need for a brief soft inhalation. After a few months the experience decayed to weekly intervals of 1-2 second periods and then disappeared altogether.

At about this time an expert relayed the apocryphal but allegedly true story of a woman troubled by more frequent and obnoxious smells who was cured by smelling her favorite odor, violets. Unfortunately it was quite inconvenient to constantly carry violets, so much later her doctor suggested that enough time had passed that she should try imagining the smell of violets instead, a cure that allegedly worked. Thus it is reasonable to conjecture that if hallucinations are sufficiently avoided by any strategy, they may eventually weaken and vanish; this is presumably already well established in the literature.

One final observation concerning cognition and the image synthesizing skill of cortex: our visual experience seems to evolve with age in largely unnoticed ways. In this case the evidence is again poorly calibrated but was persuasive to DHS. While an adolescent he stopped to stare at a tall pine tree and noticed the personally unprecedented extreme visual three-dimensional reality of its trunk, branches, and needles, a degree of improved sensory reality that subsequently lasted a lifetime. This was presumably enabled by the normal significant increase in synaptic density that occurs during adolescence.

Such an improvement might plausibly result for the two-stream model if the numbers of B synapses increased during adolescence, since the richness of the B-stream information is speculated to be a direct reflection of the richness of the cognitive experience. A second requirement for such an improvement would be a noticeable increase in the richness of the stored or memorized image set from which the complex visual field is synthesized in real time; this might reasonably be manifest as an increase in synapse numbers during such an adolescent growth event.

A possible test of this hypothesis is to compare the perceived qualities of visual realities for images that differ only in the frequency at which their underlying elements might have been viewed in preceding years. For example, suburbanites might be more sensitized to trees while city dwellers might be more sensitized to buildings.

To partially test this hypothesis an experiment of uncertain merit was devised. A suburban subject with 20-20 vision stares from a distance of perhaps six feet at an interesting tree with an exposed trunk having branches and fine leaves or needles. After realism peaks the subject then tilts perhaps 30 degrees to one side and views the same scene until realism again peaks. The hypothesis being tested would predict that if the tilted view was rare in previous years its perceived reality would be reduced. Personal observations suggest that the tilted view is sometimes perceived as less "real" than the normal view, depending on the person and the scene.

One implication is that what one repeatedly views can partially determine how vitally real it can seem, and that those who never see woods or other categories of objects may never have the same appreciation of them that others may have, simply because they don't perceive them in "three-dimensional high definition." Similar differences may also distinguish the musically or physically talented from others partly because their cognitive system has a richer set of B synapses in those cortical areas due to talent and training.

Hopefully the suggestive clues in this section concerning WVA, illusions, hallucinations, and perception may help others devise more revealing experiments that can accelerate understanding of how the brain computes and perceives and how that learning might advance medicine.

Chapter 7
Summary and conclusions

In addition to the summary of conclusions presented in Section 4.1, more speculative hypotheses include:

1) Cognons using the feedback mechanisms summarized in Section 4.1 can convey high-quality spike-based information about perceived reality downward through multiple neuron layers toward the sensors so that it can be compared at many of these layers with the upward-moving sensory information and then be used to update current perceptions at rates above ~5 Hz. This is consistent with the brain's observed ability to construct ultra-realistic three-dimensional images and to conceal blind spots by utilizing spatially adjacent information.

2) Synapses in multiple-layer dual-flow neural networks can be trained sequentially layer by layer, beginning at the sensory end and alternating between synapses that feed information upward and then those that feed information downward. Once a basic synaptic and hierarchical feature framework is established bottom to top, then it should be editable throughout life, and the synapse ratio B/A might increase with age.

3) Those neural layers or regions having superior perceptual models of the organism's external and internal sensory environment will presumably radiate more neurons toward less potent layers and regions than they receive from them, e.g., from superior conscious perception toward inferior informative regions such as the eyes.

4) The mechanism of hypotheses (1-3) also appears applicable to the training and operation of inter-cortical communications links made via white matter, where the evolving correlations among various pairs of

cortical regions should be conceptually and computationally similar to the life-long evolving correlations between each sensory system and its upper cognitive layers.

5) Hypothesis (3) further suggests that neuroanatomy may provide clues as to the hierarchical locus of consciousness since those regions nearer the core of consciousness would presumably radiate outward proportionately more white-matter neurons and synapses than they receive from more peripheral elements. It seems reasonable to expect that this core of consciousness might span many cortical and other regions.

6) Strong feedback appears to offer at least four opportunities to improve perception by helping to: a) recognize pattern sequences, b) improve signal-to-noise ratios for sensed signals, c) enable source data compression so that fewer synapses are required, and d) offer the functionality of an associative or content-addressable memory.

7) Waking visual anomalies (WVA) appear capable of providing useful clues regarding human visual system signal characteristics at neural layers that are temporarily slow to function correctly upon waking, which would seem more likely in subjects over 70 years of age. Unfortunately, deriving such information requires a subject's nearly instant recognition of the rare event and then memorization of its more neurologically informative characteristics.

8) Instant temporary termination of objectionable weak hallucinations appears to be practical using sensory signals that are sufficiently strong that they can increase the strength of the error signal sent upward so as to successfully lock perception to reality. Examples include music that terminates false voices, viewed objects that end weak visual hallucinations, and strong smells that terminate olfactory hallucinations.

Appendix A
Derivation of L, the information stored per neuron

This derivation elaborates on the summary derivation presented in Section 3.2. The recoverable information stored in a neuron, an average of L bits over an ensemble of such neurons, imperfectly characterizes which w input excitation patterns that neuron saw during training while plastic and learning-ready. Each pattern is independently selected for training from a universe of size z, where the known probability of training each pattern prior to maturity is:

$$p_T = \frac{w}{z} \tag{A.1}$$

The set of patterns trained represents information provided by a particular environment, which is characterized by the random vector $\bar{X} \in \Omega$, where the number of possible environments $|\Omega| = 2^z$ and:

$$\bar{X}_i, 1 \leq i \leq z = \begin{cases} 1, & \text{if pattern } i \text{ is taught} \\ 0, & \text{else} \end{cases} \tag{A.2}$$

The information L is extracted by observing the mature neuron's responses to all z patterns, where:

$$\bar{Y}_i, 1 \leq i \leq z = \begin{cases} 1, & \text{if pattern } i \text{ produces a spike after maturity} \\ 0, & \text{else} \end{cases} \tag{A.3}$$

$$L = I_1 z = L = I_1 z = I[\bar{X}, \bar{Y}] = I[\bar{X}_i, \bar{Y}_i] z \leq H[\bar{X}_i] z \tag{A.4}$$

I_1 is the average information provided by a single pattern in set of z, $H[\bar{X}_i]$ is the entropy of $\bar{X}_i$, $w \ll z$, and we either know for the SA model, or reasonably assume for the SS model, that the pattern learning sequence does not materially change L for the reasons discussed earlier. Moreover the learned patterns are uncorrelated for the SA model because all synapse weights equal unity during learning, and in the SS model the modest correlations between the sparse learned patterns $\overline{Y}_i$ do not materially change the result L since $w \ll z$, also as discussed earlier.

To simplify the notation, let $\overline{X}_i \equiv x$ and $\overline{Y}_i \equiv y$. Then from (A.4) and the definition of mutual information in equation (1) we have:

$$L = z \sum_{x \in \{0,1\}, y \in \{0,1\}} p_{XY}(x,y)[\log_2 p_{XY}(x,y) - \log_2 p_X(x) - \log_2 p_Y(y)] \tag{A.5}$$

where the marginal distributions of x and y follow:

$$p_X(0) = 1 - p_T, \quad p_X(1) = p_T \tag{A.6}$$

The conditional probabilities are:

$$p_{Y|X}(1|0) = p_F, \quad p_{Y|X}(1|1) = p_L \tag{A.7, A.8}$$

where p_L denotes the "learning" probability that a pattern taught to the neuron is learned (fires), p_F denotes the "false-alarm" probability that an untrained pattern is learned, and:

$$\begin{aligned} p_Y(0) &= p_{Y|X}(0|0)p_X(0) + p_{Y|X}(0|1)p_X(1) \\ &= (1-p_F)(1-p_T) + (1-p_L)p_T \end{aligned} \tag{A.9}$$

$$\begin{aligned} p_Y(1) &= p_{Y|X}(1|0)p_X(0) + p_{Y|X}(1|1)p_X(1) \\ &= p_F(1-p_T) + p_L p_T \end{aligned} \tag{A.10}$$

The sum in (A.5) can be divided into four terms t_k for which:

$$p_{XY}(0,0) = p_{Y|X}(0|0)p_X(0) = (1-p_F)(1-p_T) \tag{A.11}$$

$$p_{XY}(0,1) = p_{Y|X}(1|0)p_X(0) = p_F(1-p_T) \tag{A.12}$$

$$p_{XY}(1,0) = p_{Y|X}(0|1)p_X(1) = (1-p_L)p_T \tag{A.13}$$

$$p_{XY}(1,1) = p_{Y|X}(1|1)p_X(1) = p_L p_T \tag{A.14}$$

and:

$$t_1 = zp_{XY}(0,0)[\log_2 p_{XY}(0,0) - \log_2 p_X(0) - \log_2 p_Y(0)]$$
$$= z(1-p_F)(1-p_T)\{\log_2(1-p_F) - \log_2[(1-p_F)+(p_F-p_L)p_T]\}$$

(A.15)

after algebraic simplification. Invoking Taylor's Theorem the final term of (A.15) becomes:

$$\log_2[(1-p_F)+(p_F-p_L)p_T] \cong \log_2(1-p_F) + \frac{(p_F-p_L)p_T}{(1-p_F)\ln 2}$$

(A.16)

After simplification using (A.1) and (A.16), (A.15) becomes:

$$t_1 \cong \frac{-z(1-p_T)(p_F-p_L)p_T}{\ln 2} = \frac{w}{\ln 2}(1-p_T)(p_L-p_F)$$

(A.17)

where w is the number of patterns taught. The remaining three terms involving equations (A.12) - (A.14) can be similarly simplified using Taylor's Theorem:

$$t_2 \cong -\frac{w}{\ln 2}(1-p_T)(p_L-p_F)$$

(A.18)

$$t_3 \cong \frac{w}{\ln 2}\frac{(1-p_L)}{(1-p_F)}[\log_2(1-p_L) - \log_2(1-p_F) - (p_F-p_L)p_T]$$

(A.19)

$$t_4 \cong \frac{w}{\ln 2}\frac{p_L}{p_F}[\log_2 p_L - \log_2 p_F - (p_L-p_F)p_T]$$

(A.20)

Noting that $p_T \ll p_L$ and $p_T \ll p_F$ and summing the four terms (A.17) - (A.20) yields:

$$L \cong w\left[\log_2 \frac{1-p_L}{1-p_F} + p_L \log_2 \frac{(1-p_F)p_L}{(1-p_L)p_F}\right]$$

(A.21)

This suggests the important result that the recallable Shannon information L (bits/neuron) = 0 if $p_F \geq p_L$.

Appendix B
Basic and Extended Neuron Simulator Description

B.1 Overview

The simulator used for the presented results is written in C++ using the C++ Standard Template Library (STL) for simplicity and OpenMP for parallel performance, and it operates in a standard Linux environment. It has also been built and run on Windows in a cygwin environment. More complete source code listings and any updated versions are available for download from *http://cognon.net* or from the second author[1]. The CB neuron learning simulator trains and tests an ensemble of neurons having given parameters and reports the average results for various parameters, such as the average and standard deviation of the probability of learning, the probability of false positives (false alarms), and the learned information. The full set of collected statistics that may be reported is contained in the code in the class NeuronStatistics, which is declared in compat.h.

The CB time-domain neuron simulator uses two key classes of variables: neurons and words. Each neuron has S_o synapses, each of which has a strength value that is set to either unity or G prior to being exposed to each new word vector, and also a boolean vector "frozen" value of dimension S_o which is used only for the synapse atrophy (SA) variant of the CE neural model introduced in Chapter 3. Initially, all synapses have strength one. A word contains a list of those input synapses that fired for the most recent given excitation pattern, and a single neuron matrix corresponds to a chronological list of words, one per excitation pattern presented to that neuron.

---

[1] *Carl Staelin may be reached via email at staelin@acm.org. His personal website is http://member.acm.org/~staelin*

The pseudo-code for both words and simple neurons along with the routines "expose" and "train" are shown here:

```
struct word {
  vector<int> offset;
};
struct neuron {
 double H;
 int S;
 vector <double> strength;
};
bool expose(word* w, neuron* n) {
  double sum = 0.0;
  // Compute the weighted sum of the firing inputs
  for (int i = 0; i < w->offset.size(); ++i) {
    sum += n->strength[w->offset[i]];
  }
  if (n->H <= sum + epsilon) return true;
  return false;
}
bool train(word* w, neuron* n, double G) {
  if (expose(w, n) == false) return false;
  // Set the strength for participating synapses to G
  for (int i = 0; i < w->offset.size(); ++i) {
    n->strength[w->offset[i]] = G;
  }
  return true;
}
```

Expose models how the neuron reacts to excitation patterns, and how it computes whether or not to fire. This is embedded within an envelope that calls this code. Expose computes the weighted sum of the input word, and the neuron fires if that sum meets or exceeds a threshold. The weighted sum is the sum of the S_o element-by-element products of the most recent neuron vector, the current word, and the neuron frozen Boolean vector. The firing threshold is increased slightly by "epsilon" to avoid effects of rounding and representational errors in floating point arithmetic.

To train a neuron, "train" is called for each word to be recognized. If the neuron fires for that word then all synapses that contributed to that firing have their strengths irreversibly increased to G. Once training is complete the neuron's threshold value H is set to $H \cdot G$ by the external code which also hosts the neuron model parameters R and w, where $1/R$ is defined as the fraction of the words for which each synapse independently fires, and w is the number of words to be exposed to the neuron during training.

B.2 Description: CE spike-processing neuron time-domain simulator

The key classes are Learn, Neuron, Word, and Wordset. Important supporting classes include NeuronConfig, TrainConfig, Statistic, Histogram, and NeuronStatistics. Word contains a sparse representation of the active synapses in the input word. Wordset is simply an array of words, which may also store information regarding the delay slot learned for the word during training. Learn is an abstract class which is used during training to modify the neuron. There are currently two implementations, one for the synapse strength model and one for the synapse atrophy model.

The word class is defined as:

```
typedef vector<pair<int32, int32> > Word;
```

where vector<> and pair<> are standard STL classes.

The declaration of the Wordset class is:

```
class Wordset {
 public:
  Wordset();
  virtual ~Wordset() { }

  // Configure the wordset
  void Config(int32 num_words, int32 word_length,
              int32 num_delays, int32 refractory);
  void ConfigFixed(int32 num_words, int32 word_length,
                   int32 num_delays, int32 num_active);

  // Copy the configuration from anther wordset,
  // except for num_words.
  //
  void CopyFrom(int32 num_words, const Wordset& other);

  // Randomize word vector according to configuration
  virtual void Init();
```

```cpp
    const int32 size() const { return words_.size(); }
    void set_size(int32 num_words);

    int32 word_length() const { return word_length_; }
    int32 num_delays() const { return num_delays_; }

    const Word& get_word(int32 i) const {
      return words_[i];
    }
    void set_word(int32 i, const Word& word) {
      words_[i] = word;
    }

    // get/set the trained delay slot for a given word
    int32 delay(int32 word) const;
    int32 set_delay(int32 word, int32 delay);

    // get/set the refractory period
    int32 refractory() const { return refractory_; }
    void set_refractory(int32 refractory) {
      refractory_ = refractory;
    }

    // get/set number of active signals for a given word
    int32 num_active() const { return num_active_; }
    void set_num_active(int32 num_active) {
      num_active_ = num_active;
    }

  protected:
    int num_words_;     // Number of words
    int word_length_;   // Length of words (#synapses)
    int num_delays_;    // Number of delays
    int refractory_;    // Refractory period
    int num_active_;    // Number of active signals
    vector<Word> words_;
    vector<int32> delays_;
    scoped_ptr<RandomBase> random_;   // Random number
                                      // generator

    void InitOrig();
    void InitFixed();
};
```

Normal usage is to create a Wordset, configure the wordset via either Config() or ConfigFixed(), which imply different methods of randomly initializing each word and will be described more fully later, Init() the Wordset to randomize the word, and then get word() to get words to pass to the neuron for training or recognition.

The Neuron class declaration:

```
class Neuron {
 public:
  Neuron();
  virtual ~Neuron() { }

  // Initializes a neuron
  virtual void Init(const NeuronConfig& config);

  // Expose a neuron to a word.
  //
  // A word is a random vector of
  // [0, ..., d1-1, kDisabled] values, with
  // non-disabled values on average every R slots.
  //
  int32 Expose(const Word& word);

  // Train a neuron to recognize a word.
  //
  // A word is a random vector of
  // [0, ..., d1-1, kDisabled] values, with
  // non-disabled values on average every R slots.
  //
  int32 Train(const Word& word);

  // Start a new training cycle.
  void StartTraining();

  // Finished a training cycle, so update synapses and
  // statistics as appropriate.
  //
  void FinishTraining();

  // Accumulate histograms
  //
  // histogram: histogram of delays that could fire
```

```cpp
        // max_histogram: histogram of delay with maximum
        //                firing sum
        // H_histogram: histogram of container summation
        //                values
        //
        void GetInputDelayHistogram(const Word& word,
                            vector<int32>* histogram,
                            vector<int32>* max_histogram,
                            vector<int32>* H_histogram);

        void GetSynapseDelayHistogram(
                            vector<int32>* histogram);

        // Various functions to report the Neuron's
        // configuration
        //
        const NeuronConfig& config() { return config_; }
        const int32 C() const { return C_; }
        const int32 D1() const { return D1_; }
        const int32 D2() const { return D2_; }
        const int32 slots() const { return (D1_ + D2_); }
        const double H() const { return H_; }
        const double Q() const { return Q_; }
        const double Q_after() const { return Q_after_; }
        const int32 R() const { return R_; }
        const double G_m() const { return G_m_; }
        const double H_m() const { return H_m_; }
        const int32 length() const { return length_; }

        void set_H(double value) { H_ = value; }

        const int32 delays(int i) const {
          return delays_[i];
        }
        void set_delays(int i, int32 value) {
          delays_[i] = value;
        }

        const int32 containers(int i) const {
          return containers_[i];
```

```cpp
  }
  void set_containers(int i, int32 value) {
    containers_[i] = value;
  }

  const bool frozen(int i) const { return frozen_[i]; }
  void set_frozen(int i, bool value) {
    frozen_[i] = value;
  }

  const double strength(int i) const {
    return strength_[i];
  }
  void set_strength(int i, double value) {
    strength_[i] = value;
  }

private:
  NeuronConfig config_;   // Configuration data
  int32 C_;               // Number of containers
  int32 D1_;              // Number of input delays
  int32 D2_;              // Number of axon delays
  double H_;              // Firing threshold
  double Q_;              // Oversampling rates
  double Q_after_;        // Q after training
  int32 R_;               // Refractory period
  double G_m_;            // Increment synapse strength by
                          // this amount
  double H_m_;            // Synapse-strength threshold value

  scoped_ptr<RandomBase> random_;  // Pointer to random
                                   // number generator
  int32 length_;                   // The # of synapses
  vector<int32> delays_;           // The delay for each
                                   // synapse
  vector<int32> containers_;       // The container id for
                                   // each synapse
  vector<bool> frozen_;            // Is the synapse frozen?
  vector<double> strength_;        // Strength of the
                                   // synapse
```

```
    vector<double> sum_;          // Per container
                                  // summation values
    scoped_ptr<Learn> learn_;     // Modifies neuron during
                                  // learning
};
```

Normal usage would be to create a neuron, initialize it with a configuration using Init(), prepare it for learning via StartTraining(), train it on a number of words with Train(), complete the training using FinishTraining(), and then use it to recognize words with Expose().

Neuron uses a pointer to a hidden abstract class, Learn, to manage the training using the member variable learn_. Currently there are two implementations of Learn, one for synapse atrophy training and one for synapse strength. Neuron's Init() function examines the requested neuron configuration and instantiates an instance of the appropriate Learn implementation.

The declaration of the abstract base class Learn is:

```
class Learn {
 public:
  explicit Learn(Neuron* neuron);
  virtual ~Learn();

  virtual void StartTraining() = 0;
  virtual void UpdateSynapse(int synapse) = 0;
  virtual void FinishTraining() = 0;
 protected:
  Neuron* neuron_;
};
```

Learn is used by Neuron as follows. StartTraining is called before training begins, to ensure that the neuron is ready to learn. During training, UpdateSynapse is called once for each synapse that participated in the neuron firing. FinishTraining is called when training is complete to prepare the neuron for the recognition phase.

The implementations of synapse strength learning is contained sub-class LearnSynapseStrength, whose implementation is:

```
void LearnSynapseStrength::StartTraining() {
```

```
    neuron_->set_H(neuron_->config().h());
}

void LearnSynapseStrength::UpdateSynapse(int synapse) {
    neuron_->set_strength(synapse,
                          neuron_->config().g_m());
    neuron_->set_frozen(synapse, true);
}

void LearnSynapseStrength::FinishTraining() {
    neuron_->set_H(neuron_->config().h_m());
}
```

StartTraining ensures that the firing threshold is set to the lower training value. UpdateSynapse simply sets the synapse strength to G, the gain. FinishTraining updates the firing threshold to the higher recognition threshold.

Synapse atrophy training is implemented in LearnSynapseAtrophy, whose implementation is:

```
void LearnSynapseAtrophy::StartTraining() { }

void LearnSynapseAtrophy::UpdateSynapse(int synapse) {
    neuron_->set_frozen(synapse, true);
}

void LearnSynapseAtrophy::FinishTraining() {
    for (int32 i = 0; i < neuron_->length(); ++i) {
        if (!neuron_->frozen(i)) {
            neuron_->set_strength(i, 0.0);
            neuron_->set_delays(i, kDisabled);
        }
    }
}
```

StartTraining is unecessary for this learning method, so it has an empty implementation. UpdateSynapse simply "freezes" each synapse that participates in learning, which marks it as having been used in training so it won't be disabled when training completes.. FinishTraining atrophies unused synapses to zero by marking them disabled.

Neurons are initialized randomly as follows:

```
void Neuron::Init(const NeuronConfig& config) {
  // Intialize neuron values
  config_ = config;
  C_  = config.c();
  D1_ = config.d1();
  D2_ = config.d2();
  H_  = config.h();
  Q_  = config.q();
  R_  = config.r();
  Q_after_ = -1.0;
  if (config.has_g_m()) {
    G_m_ = config.g_m();
  } else {
    G_m_ = -1.0;
  }
  if (config.has_h_m()) {
    H_m_ = config.h_m();
  } else {
    H_m_ = -1.0;
  }
  length_ = static_cast<int32>(floor(C_ * H_ * Q_ * R_
                                     + kEpsilon));

  // Initialize each synapses' delay, container, and
  // frozen status
  //
  if (delays_.size() != length_) {
    delays_.resize(length_);
    containers_.resize(length_);
    frozen_.resize(length_);
    strength_.resize(length_);
    sum_.resize(C_);
  }

  // Randomly assign delays and containers to each
  // synapse
```

122

```
  //
  for (int32 i = 0; i < length_; ++i) {
    // Randomly assign delays to synapses
    delays_[i] = random_->Rand32() % D2_;
    // Randomly assign synapses to containers
    containers_[i] = random_->Rand32() % C_;
    frozen_[i] = false;
    strength_[i] = 1.0;
  }

  if (config.has_g_m() && config.has_h_m()) {
    learn_.reset(new LearnSynapseStrength(this));
  } else {
    learn_.reset(new LearnSynapseAtrophy(this));
  }
}
```

Expose is the heart of the model, and it simply computes whether the neuron summation met or exceeded the threshold.

```
int32 Neuron::Expose(const Word& word) {
  // Iterate over delays checking whether occurs
  int s = slots();
  for (int32 d = 0; d < s; ++d) {
    for (int32 i = 0; i < C_; ++i) {
      sum_[i] = 0.0;
    }
    // Iterate over sparse signals in word
    for (Word::const_iterator it = word.begin();
         it != word.end(); ++it) {
      int32 synapse = it->first;
      int32 delay = it->second;

      // If delay and word delay adds up to current
      // delay then increment the container's sum by
      // that synapse's strength.
      //
      if (delays_[synapse] + delay == d) {
        sum_[containers_[synapse]] +=
            strength_[synapse];
      }
```

```
  }

  // Iterate through containers to see if any fired
  for (int32 i = 0; i < C_; ++i) {
    // If at least H firings, then denote that
    // container as fired.
    //
    if (H_ <= sum_[i] + kEpsilon) return d;
  }
  }
  return kDisabled;
}
```

First, it iterates through the active synapses in the input word (which is usually sparse), computing the summation within each compartment independently in the member vector sum_. Then it checks each compartment to see if any of them should have fired.

Train is the routine which trains a neuron given an input word.

```
int32 Neuron::Train(const Word& word) {
  int32 d = Expose(word);

  if (d == kDisabled) return d;

  // Iterate through containers to see which fired
  for (int32 i = 0; i < C_; ++i) {
    if (sum_[i] + kEpsilon < H_) continue;
    // Update those synapses that contributed to the
    // neuron firing.
    //
    for (Word::const_iterator it = word.begin();
         it != word.end(); ++it) {
      int32 synapse = it->first;
      int32 delay = it->second;

      if (delays_[synapse] + delay == d
          && containers_[synapse] == i) {
        learn_->UpdateSynapse(synapse);
      }
```

```
        }
        break;
    }
    return d;
}
```

First it checks to see if the neuron fired. If it didn't, then there is nothing to learn, so it returns. If it did fire then it determines which compartment, or compartments, caused the neuron to fire, and updates each synapse which participated in the firing. This implementation becomes somewhat inefficient if both C and the probability of learning p_L are large because if multiple containers fired, all participating synapses in those firing compartments are strengthened whereas one compartment would suffice. Experiments testing independent learning by compartments under natural conditions would be very helpful in refining the extended cognon (CE) model.

References

Averbeck, B. B., Latham, P. E., & Pouget, A. (2006). Neural correlations, population coding and computation. *Nature Reviews Neuroscience*, 7, 358–366.

Baldassi, C., Braunstein, A., Brunel, N. & Zecchina, R. (2007). Efficient supervised learning in networks with binary synapses. *Proceedings of the National Academy of Sciences (PNAS)*, 104(26), 11079–11084.

Barrett A. B. & van Rossum, M. C. W. (2008). Optimal learning rules for discrete synapses. *Public Library of Science (PLoS) Computation Biology*, 4(11), 1–7.

Berger, T. (2003). Living information theory (the 2002 Shannon Lecture). *IEEE Information Theory Society Newsletter, 53*(1), 1, 6–19.

Berger, T. & Levy, W. B. (2010). A mathematical theory of energy efficient neural computation and communication. *IEEE Transactions on Information Theory*, 56(2), 652–874.

Bi, G.-Q. & Poo, M.-M. (1998). Synaptic modifications in cultured hippocampal neurons: dependence on spike timing, synaptic strength, and postsynaptic cell type. *Journal of Neuroscience*, 18, 10464–10472.

Bloom, B. H. (1970). Space/time trade-offs in hash coding with allowable errors. *Communications of the Association for Computing Machinery (ACM)*, 13(7), 422–426, doi:10.1145/362686.362692.

Blum, A. L. & Rivest, R. L. (1992). Training a 3-node neural network is NP-complete. *Neural Networks*, 5, 117–127.

Bohte, S. M. (2004). The evidence for neural information processing with precise spike-times: A survey. *Natural Computing*, 3(2), 195–206.

Braitenberg, V. & Schuz, A. (1998). *Cortex: statistics and geometry of neuronal connectivity*. Berlin: Springer-Verlag.

Branco, T., Clark, B. A., & Hausser, M. (2010). Dendritic discrimination of temporal input sequences in cortical neurons. *Science, 329*(5999), 1671–1675.

Brown, E. M., Kass, R. E., & Mitra, P. P. (2004). Multiple neural spike train data analysis: state-of-the-art and future challenges. *Nature Neuroscience*, 7(5), 456–461.

Buesing L. & Maass, W. (2010). A spiking neuron as information bottleneck. *Neural Computation, 22*(8), 1961–1992.

Coleman, T. P. & Sarma, S. S. (2010). A computationally efficient method for nonparametric modeling of neural spiking activity with point processes. *Neural Computation, 22(8), 2002–2030.*

Davidson, T. J., Kloosterman, F. & Wilson, M. A. (2009) Hippocampal replay of extended experience, *Neuron*, 63 (4), 497-507.

Freiwald, W. A. & Tsao, D. Y. (2010). Functional compartmentalization and viewpoint generalization within the macaque face-processing system. *Science*, 330(6005), 845–851.

Gollisch, T. & Meister, M. (2008). Rapid neural coding in the retina with relative spike latencies. *Science*, 319(5866), 1108–1111.

Hawkins, J. & Blakeslee, S. (2004). *On Intelligence.* New York, NY: Henry Holt and Company.

Hopfield, J. J. (1982). Neural networks and physical systems with emergent collective computational abilities. *Proceedings of the National Academy of Sciences* (PNAS), 79, 2554–2558.

Hopfield, J. J. & Brody, C. D. (2004). Learning rules and network repair in spike-timing-based computation networks. *Proceedings of the National Academy of Sciences* (PNAS), 101, 337–342.

Hopfield, J. J., Brody, C. D., & Roweis, S. (1998). Computing with action potentials. In M. I. Jordan, M. J. Kearns, & S. A. Solla (Eds.), *Advances in Neural Information Processing Systems 10: Proceedings of the 11th Annual Conference on Neural Information Processing* (pp. 166-172). Cambridge, MA: MIT Press.

Koch, C. (1999). *Biophysics of Computation: Information Processing in Single Neurons.* Oxford: Oxford University Press.

Koch, C. (2004). *The Quest for Conciousness: A Neurobiological Approach.* Englewood CO., Roberts & Company.

Kozhevnikov, A. A. & Fee, M. S. (2007). Singing-related activity of identified HVC neurons in the zebra finch. *Journal of Neurophysiology*, 97(6), 4271–4283.

Linsker, R. (1989). How to generate ordered maps by maximizing the mutual information between input and output signals. *Neural Computation, 1*(3), 402–411.

London, M. & Hausser, M. (2005). Dendritic computation. *Review of Neuroscience*, 28, 503–532.

Malvar, H. S. and Staelin, D. H. (1989). The LOT: transform coding without blocking effects. *IEEE Trans. Acoustics, Speech, and Signal Proc.*, *37* (4), 553-559.

Markram, H., Lubke, J., Frotscher, M., & Sakmann, B. (1997). Regulation of synaptic efficacy by coincidence of postsynaptic APs and EPSPs. *Science*, 275(5297), 213–215.

McCulloch, W. S. & Pitts, W. (1943). A logical calculus of the ideas immanent in nervous activity. *Bulletin of Mathematical Biology*, 5(4), 115–133.

Milner, B., Squire, L. R., & Kandel, E. R. (1998). Cognitive neuroscience and the study of memory. *Neuron*, 20, 445–468.

Panatier, A., Theodosis, D. T., Mothet, J.-P., Touquet, B., Pollegioni, L., Poulain, D. A., & Oliet, S. H. R. (2006). Glia-derived D-serine controls NMDA receptor activity and synaptic memory. *Cell*, 125(4), 775–784.

Parra, L. C., Beck, J. M., & Bell, A. J. (2009). On the maximization of information flow between spiking neurons," *Neural Computation, 21*(11), 2991–3009.

Quiroga, R. Q. & Panzeri, S. (2009). Extracting information from neuronal populations: information theory and decoding approaches. *Nature Reviews Neuroscience, 10*, 173–185.

Rall, W. (1977). Core conductor theory and cable properties of neurons. In E. R. Kandel, J. M. Brookhardt, & V. B. Mountcastle (Eds.), *Handbook of Physiology, Section 1: The Nervous System, Volume 1, Cellular Biology of Neurons, Part 1* (pp. 39–97). Bethesda, MD: American Physiological Society.

Rieke, F., Warland, D., de Ruyter van Steveninck, R. R., & Bialek, W. (1996). *Spikes: exploring the neural code.* Cambridge, MA: MIT Press.

Shannon, C.E. (1948). A mathematical theory of communication, *Bell System Technical Journal, 27*, 379-423 and 623-656.

Sjostrom, P. J. & Hausser, M. (2006). A cooperative switch determines the sign of synaptic plasticity in distal dendrites of neocortical pyramidal neurons. *Neuron*, 51, 227–238.

Stickgold, R., Malia, A., Maguire, D., Roddenberry, D., & O'Connor, M. (2000). Replaying the game: hyponagogic images in normals and amnesics, *Science*, *290*, 350-353.

Stickgold, R. (2005). Sleep-dependent memory consolidation. *Nature*, *437*, 1272-1277.

Thorpe, S., Fize, D., & Marlot, C. (1996). Speed of processing in the human visual system. *Nature*, 381, 520–522.

VanRullen, R., Guyonneau, R., & Thorpe, S. J. (2005). Spike times make sense. *Trends in Neurosciences*, 28(1), 1–4.

Volterra, A. & Meldolesi, J. (2005). Astrocytes, from brain glue to communication elements: the revolution continues. *Nature Reviews Neuroscience*, *6*, 626–640.

Willshaw, D. J., Buneman, O. P., & Longuet-Higgins, H. C. (1969). Non-holographic associative memory. *Nature*, *222*, 960–964.

Zheng, P., Tang, W., & Zhang, J. (2010). Efficient continuous-time asymmetric Hopfield networks for memory retrieval. *Neural Computation*, 22(6), 1597–1614.

Acknowledgements

The authors thank J. Lim for his support of K. T. Herring, who helped select mutual information as the appropriate Shannon learning metric and who contributed most of the derivation of the mutual information expression presented in Appendix A. The authors also thank Google for supporting the second author's work as it neared completion. We are also grateful to our many MIT colleagues for useful discussions over many decades concerning these same problems including, in chronological order: J. Weisner, W. Pitts, W. McCulloch, M. Minsky, S. Mason, T. Welch, D. Freeman, T. Poggio, M. Wilson, S. Mitter, and S. J. Keyser. In addition, the time, effort, and thought of our test readers is greatly appreciated, and this monograph is better for their efforts. We should also like to thank our families for their support during this effort, which often took time from them.

About the Authors

David Staelin is Professor Emeritus in the Department of Electrical Engineering and Computer Science at the Massachusetts Institute of Technology (MIT) where he actively served on the faculty for 46 years and also received his SB, SM, and ScD degrees. His teaching involves signal processing, estimation, and electromagnetics, and his recent research has primarily involved neural signal processing, remote sensing and estimation, image processing, and communications networks. Neural spike processing has been an interest for over 50 years and became a major effort in 2007. He was an Assistant Director of the MIT Lincoln Laboratory from 1990 to 2001, a member of the (U.S.) President's Information Technology Advisory Committee 2003-2005, and founding Chairman of PictureTel Corporation, now part of Polycom.

Carl Staelin is a member of the technical staff at Google, Israel and an assistant editor for the Journal of Electronic Imaging. Earlier he was Chief Technologist for Hewlett Packard Labs Israel, working on automatic image analysis and processing, digital commercial print, and enterprise IT management. His research interests include digital storage systems, machine learning, image analysis and processing, document and information management, and computer performance analysis. He received his PhD in Computer Science from Princeton University in high performance file system design. He currently lives in Haifa, Israel with his wife and family.